# Note from the Publisher

## What this book is not

### This book is NOT the BIBLE

Now before you roll your eyes and say something like 'duh,' let me explain. This book is not the Bible because nothing else can be like God's Holy Bible. It is unique in all of creation and humanity. That is to say, among all things written or communicated, since time began, the Bible stands alone.

From a human perspective, it was written over a span of about 1,500 years, by around 40 different authors, completing its 66 different books. But it's really better to think of these writers as participants in the process and not the actual writers, themselves. The true author of the Bible is the Holy Spirit, which is why we often see or hear the Bible referred to as "The Inspired Word of God."

God Himself moved, or *inspired*, people of His choosing to pen and compile the Holy Scriptures. 2 Timothy 3:16 tells us that "All Scripture is God-breathed" (Berean Standard version), or "is given by inspiration of God" (King James version). So if God is the ultimate author, why are the books of the Bible so different in genre, writing style, and voice? It's because God didn't use these people merely as secretaries or transcribers. It was His Holy Spirit that guided and controlled what they wrote, but each of the writers naturally used their own vocabulary and style—some were highly educated kings while others were just everyday fishermen… but God was working through them.

So this book, The Bible Made Simple and Easy, is a sort of *primer*, or guidebook, to the real thing.

Because let's face it- The Bible can be hard to comprehend, maybe even be overwhelming, at first. But when you think about it, why wouldn't it be?

"written by around 40 different authors" … "over a span of about 1,500 years."

Add to that the different cultural backgrounds (not to mention that it was originally written in, at least, three different languages), then consider the incredible depth of content and knowledge between its pages, and it's no wonder that reading and understanding it takes effort.

But when you have a basic overview, and see how it's all connected, it's not nearly so daunting a task (and it can truly change your life).

That's where this book comes in. It is not the Bible (because nothing else is) but it can prime your knowledge for learning the actual words of God, your Creator.

**"For the word of God is living and active." Hebrews 4:12a**

# The Bible Made Simple And Easy

Copyright © 2024 by Elkleaf Publishing

All rights reserved. No part of this publication may be reproduced, distributed, or transmitted in any form or by any means, including photocopying, recording, or other electronic or mechanical methods, without the prior written permission of the publisher, except in the case of brief quotations embodied in critical reviews and certain other noncommercial uses permitted by copyright law. For permission requests, contact the publisher, with subject "Attention: Permissions" at the email address below.

Elkleaf Publishing
publisher@elkleafpublishing.com


https://elkleafpublishing.com


Elkleaf books are available at special discounts when purchased in bulk for premiums and sales promotions as well as for fund-raising or educational use. Special discounts are also available on quantity purchases by corporations, associations, churches, ministries, and others. For details, contact the publisher at the email address above.

# Contents

## Old Testament

| | | | |
|---|---|---|---|
| **ABOUT THIS BOOK** | 7 | | |
| **THE LAW** | **9** | PROVERBS | 52 |
| GENESIS | 10 | ECCLESIASTES | 54 |
| EXODUS | 12 | SONG OF SOLOMON | 56 |
| LEVITICUS | 14 | **MAJOR PROPHETS** | **59** |
| NUMBERS | 16 | ISAIAH | 60 |
| DEUTERONOMY | 18 | JEREMIAH | 62 |
| **HISTORY** | **21** | LAMENTATIONS | 64 |
| JOSHUA | 22 | EZEKIEL | 66 |
| JUDGES | 24 | DANIEL | 68 |
| RUTH | 26 | **MINOR PROPHETS** | **71** |
| 1 SAMUEL | 28 | HOSEA | 72 |
| 2 SAMUEL | 30 | JOEL | 74 |
| 1 KINGS | 32 | AMOS | 76 |
| 2 KINGS | 34 | OBADIAH | 78 |
| 1 CHRONICLES | 36 | JONAH | 80 |
| 2 CHRONICLES | 38 | MICAH | 82 |
| EZRA | 40 | NAHUM | 84 |
| NEHEMIAH | 42 | HABAKKUK | 86 |
| ESTHER | 44 | ZEPHANIAH | 88 |
| **POETRY** | **47** | HAGGAI | 90 |
| JOB | 48 | ZECHARIAH | 92 |
| PSALMS | 50 | MALACHI | 94 |

# Contents

## New Testament

| | | | |
|---|---|---|---|
| **THE GOSPELS AND ACTS** | **97** | 1 TIMOTHY | 128 |
| MATTHEW | 98 | 2 TIMOTHY | 130 |
| MARK | 100 | PHILEMON | 134 |
| LUKE | 102 | **GENERAL EPISTLES** | **137** |
| JOHN | 104 | HEBREWS | 138 |
| ACTS | 106 | JAMES | 140 |
| **PAULINE EPISTLES** | **109** | 1 PETER | 142 |
| ROMANS | 110 | 2 PETER | 144 |
| 1 CORINTHIANS | 112 | 1 JOHN | 146 |
| 2 CORINTHIANS | 114 | 2 JOHN | 148 |
| GALATIANS | 116 | 3 JOHN | 150 |
| EPHESIANS | 118 | Jude | 152 |
| PHILIPPIANS | 120 | **PROPHETIC** | **155** |
| COLOSSIANS | 122 | REVELATION | 156 |
| 1 THESSALONIANS | 124 | **Acknowledgments:** | **158** |
| 2 THESSALONIANS | 126 | **More from Elkleaf Publishing:** | **159** |

# Explore the Bible with Ease
# Two-Page Spread Summaries for All 66 Books

Navigating the breadth of the Bible can be daunting with its extensive pages and ancient texts. This handy guide simplifies each of the 66 books into concise, easy-view, two-page side-by-side summaries, tailored to provide clarity and essential insights. Perfect for anyone looking for a more approachable way to explore biblical stories and teachings, here's what this guide delivers:

- **Concise Book Summaries:** Each book of the Bible is distilled into a beautifully designed summary featuring key details such as the author, era of composition, main themes, pivotal verses, and visual aides for easier understanding.
- **Perfect for Various Needs:** Whether as a road map for personal study, group discussions, or as a heartfelt gift, these summaries serve as a helpful companion for deepening your understanding of the Scriptures.
- **Insightful Contextual Background:** More than just overviews, each summary provides context, unraveling how each book plays a part in the larger narrative of God's story—from Genesis to Revelation.
- **User-Friendly Layout:** Crafted for ease of use, this guide is ideal for anyone seeking quick insights or a refresh of their biblical knowledge, providing clarity and insight into each Biblical book in a simple and accessible way.

Enhance your exploration of the Bible today. Whether you are a new believer or a seasoned Bible student, this guide provides you with straightforward navigation in a 'connect the dots' fashion between all the books that make up God's Word.

## *With multi-color coded visual aides and beautiful graphics for a more immersive and intuitive experience.*

All scripture references within this book - to the best of the publisher's knowledge and intentions - are from either the Berean Standard Bible (BSB) or the King James Version (KJV).

**Elkleaf Publishing**

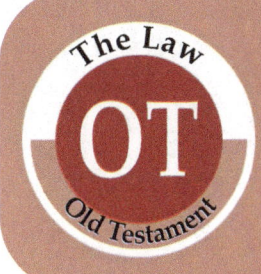 # THE LAW

# The Law
### Exodus Leviticus Genesis Numbers Deuteronomy

The first five books of the Bible, known as the Pentateuch, were composed by Moses. These foundational texts capture the origins of the universe, the creation of our world, and the inception of humanity, along with the entrance of sin. Within these pages, we encounter the first murder, the rise of false religion, the global flood, and the comforting symbol of the rainbow. They detail the destruction of Sodom and Gomorrah, the establishment of Israel as a nation, and the dramatic Exodus from Egypt, including the parting of the Red Sea.

Within the Pentateuch, we also find God's holy directives, such as the Ten Commandments, the meticulous construction of the tabernacle, and guidelines for sacrifices and worship. These books provide numerous ordinances for societal conduct and stern warnings about the importance of holiness. More profoundly, they offer our first glimpses into the nature of God, revealing His love for holiness and His hatred of sin. Here, we begin to comprehend the divine narrative woven throughout human history, shaped by God's righteous character.

The Pentateuch also brings to life historic figures like Adam and Eve, Abraham and Sarah, Jacob, Joseph, Moses, Aaron, and Joshua. These individuals become more than just names; they are central to the unfolding story of God's redemptive plan. By recording their lives, challenges, and faith in God, the Pentateuch serves as a timeless testament to God's enduring faithfulness and His desire for a holy people, guiding believers to understand and embrace His covenant promises.

**Personal Notes:**

# GENESIS

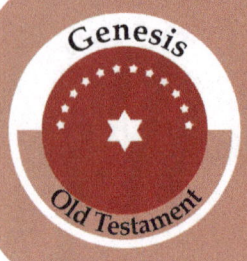

**Author:** Moses

**Time Written:** Between 1440 and 1400 B.C.

**Time Covered:** From Creation to about 1806 B.C.

Genesis, meaning "origin" in Greek and "In the beginning" in Hebrew, serves as the foundational narrative for many crucial aspects of both cosmic and human history. It details the creation of the universe, mankind, and the introduction of sin and death, as well as the initial steps in God's remarkable plan for redemption. The initial chapters of Genesis are particularly focused on the proliferation of sin, culminating in a catastrophic global flood. Within these passages, we witness the power of God's word, which He uses to create, define, and bless the cosmos, imbuing it with identity, purpose, and value. For every believer today, Genesis holds a deeply personal significance.

**A Key Verse:** Genesis 1:1, In the beginning God created the heavens and the earth.

It teaches that God crafted each of us intentionally, speaking us into existence and endowing us with unique talents and a specific purpose well before our earthly birth. Throughout our lives, God continues to call us, guiding and protecting us as His beloved children, secured by His grace. This narrative underscores the importance of recognizing and responding to God's ongoing presence and direction in our lives. The latter part of Genesis shifts focus to Abraham, through whom God promises to bring both salvation and blessings to all nations. As the patriarchs—from Abraham to Isaac, and Jacob to Joseph—hear and respond to God's promises, they experience both trials and

**A Popular Verse:** Genesis 50:20, As for you, what you intended against me for evil, God intended for good, in order to accomplish a day like this—to preserve the lives of many people.

triumphs, learning the necessity of steadfast faith in the Lord. Through these stories, Genesis not only introduces key themes of holiness, sin, and redemption but also sets the stage for the unfolding story of God's grace and mercy across the Bible, highlighting the ongoing narrative of redemption through God's covenant (or sacred promise) with His people.

**Personal Notes:**

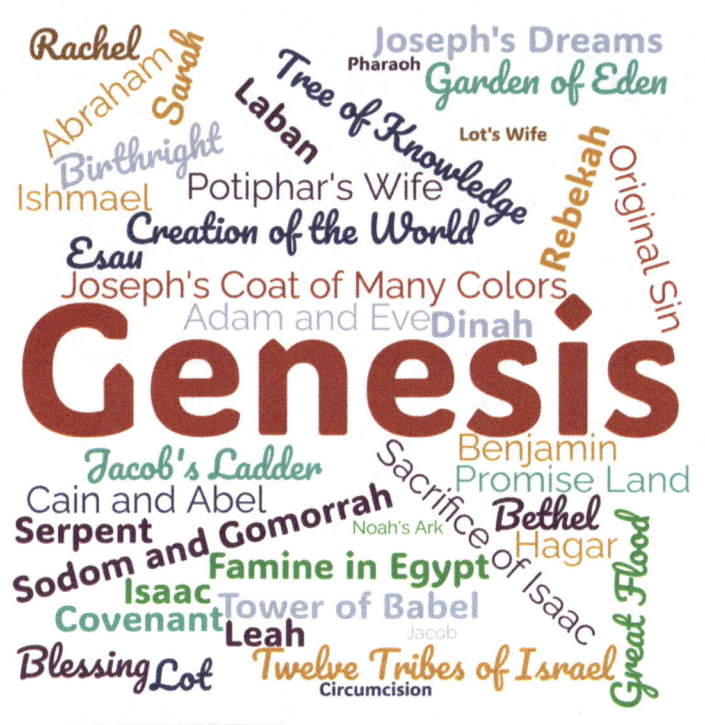

# Reflections on Genesis
*Creation and Beginnings*

Though sin marred the pristine creation of God, redemption resounded through His chosen people, the Israelites. The lives of Abraham, Isaac, and Jacob offer deep understandings of God's everlasting covenant and our aspirations for the times to come. Additionally, the narrative of Joseph and his siblings serves as a parable, illustrating the proper and improper ways we, as believers, should engage with our community and the broader world, imparting essential lessons on love, unity, and forgiveness.

## NOTABLE & POPULAR

**People**

Abraham, Adam, Noah, Jacob, Joseph

**Places**

Eden, Ararat, Ur, Bethel, Egypt

**Events**

Creation, Fall, Flood, Covenant with Abraham, Joseph's Rise

**Verses**

**Genesis 1:2** Now the earth was formless and void, and darkness was over the surface of the deep. And the Spirit of God was hovering over the surface of the waters.

**Genesis 1:3** And God said, "Let there be light," and there was light.

**Genesis 3:15** And I will put enmity between you and the woman, and between your seed and her seed. He will crush your head, and you will strike his heel. "

**Genesis 12:2-3** I will make you into a great nation, and I will bless you; I will make your name great, so that you will be a blessing. I will bless those who bless you and curse those who curse you; and all the families of the earth will be blessed through you. "

# EXODUS

**Author:** Moses

**Time Written:** Between 1440 and 1400 B.C.

**Time Covered:** Around 1800 to 1440 B.C.

The term Exodus, derived from the Greek for "exit," "departure," or "going out," encapsulates the essence of this pivotal biblical book. The Septuagint, an ancient Greek translation of the Old Testament, aligns this title with the significant event of Israel's departure from Egypt, while the New Testament references in Luke 9:31 and 2 Peter 1:15 extend its metaphor to signify the departure from life through physical death, resonating with the theme of redemption through death found in Exodus. Exodus chronicles the formation of Israel from a small family of seventy individuals in Egypt into a robust nation of two to three million by the time of their departure. This

*A Key Verse:* Exodus 20:2-3, "I am the Lord your God, who brought you out of the land of Egypt, out of the house of slavery. You shall have no other gods before Me.

transformation occurred under divine watchfulness, where God not only nurtured but also protected and sustained His people through profound struggles and growth pains. Central to this narrative is Moses, a man of humble origins and considerable self-doubt, who was raised in Egyptian royalty but called by God from a remarkably non-consuming burning bush. Despite his initial hesitance and past failures, Moses is charged by God to liberate the Israelites from the clutches of Egyptian oppression. This mission underlines the book's core themes of divine redemption and deliverance. Through Moses' leadership and the dramatic plagues that afflict Egypt

*A Popular Verse:* Exodus 3:14, God said to Moses, "I AM WHO I AM. This is what you are to say to the Israelites: 'I AM has sent me to you.'"

when Pharaoh resists God's command to free the Israelites, Exodus not only showcases God's power and justice but also His deep commitment to fulfilling His covenant promises. These aspects are vividly displayed as Moses, embracing his divine commission, leads the Israelites out of cruel bondage, setting the stage for their journey towards the promised land that God said He would give to Abraham and his descendants (Gen. 12:7).

**Personal Notes:**

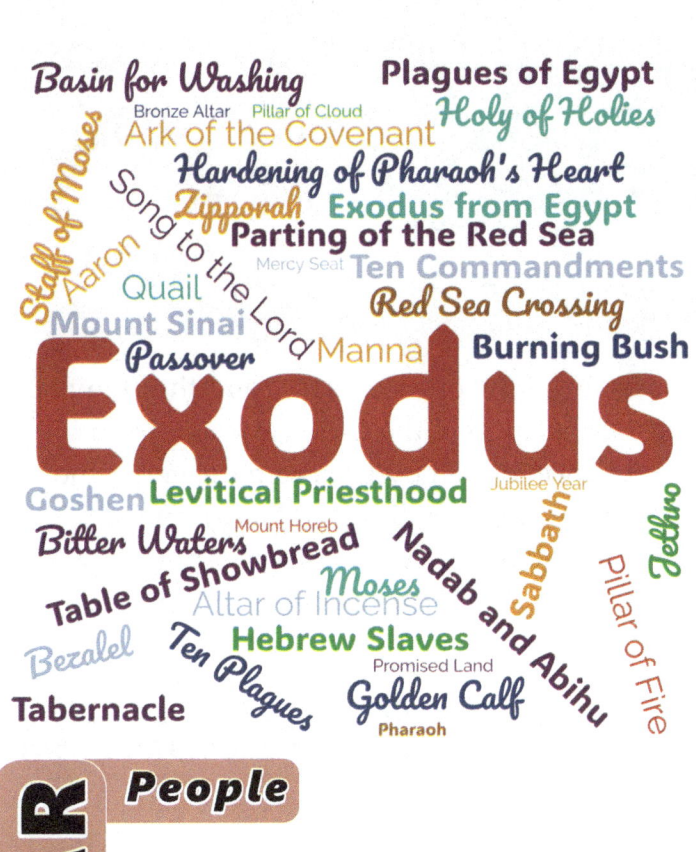

# Reflections on Exodus
*Liberation and Covenant*

In His infinite wisdom, God chose Moses to lead Israel, playing a crucial role in their liberation from Egyptian slavery. The covenant laws that Moses presented were not of his own making but divinely ordained, forming a seamless guide for living that promised blessings for God's people. Moreover, Moses' directives for Tabernacle worship, grounded in a heavenly directive, were intended to welcome God's favor, highlighting his function as a channel of divine guidance and blessings.

## NOTABLE & POPULAR

**People**

Moses, Pharaoh, Aaron, Miriam, Joshua

**Places**

Sinai, Egypt, Red Sea, Wilderness

**Events**

Plagues, Red Sea Crossing, Ten Commandments, Burning Bush

**Verses**

**Exodus 1:8** Then a new king, who did not know Joseph, came to power in Egypt.

**Exodus 2:24-25** So God heard their groaning, and He remembered His covenant with Abraham, Isaac, and Jacob. God saw the Israelites and took notice.

**Exodus 12:27** you are to reply, 'It is the Passover sacrifice to the Lord, who passed over the houses of the Israelites in Egypt when He struck down the Egyptians and spared our homes.'" Then the people bowed down and worshiped.

**Exodus 14:21** Then Moses stretched out his hand over the sea, and all that night the Lord drove back the sea with a strong east wind that turned it into dry land. So the waters were divided,

# LEVITICUS

**Author:** Moses

**Time Written:** Between 1440 and 1400 B.C

**Time Covered:** Around 1445 B.C.

Ancient Jewish writings refer to the Book of Leviticus as the "Law of the Priests" and the "Law of the Offerings," while the Greek Septuagint (the earliest translation of the Old Testament from Hebrew to Greek) names it Leuitikon, indicating its relevance to the Levites. From this term, the Latin Vulgate (an early and important 5th century version of the Holy Bible, in Latin) coined "Leviticus," the title by which it is known in all English translations. Leviticus serves as God's guidebook for Israel in the Old Testament, instructing them on the intricacies of worship, service, and obedience to maintain a holy fellowship with Him. The book notably emphasizes God's

*A Key Verse:* **Leviticus 19:18, Do not seek revenge or bear a grudge against any of your people, but love your neighbor as yourself. I am the Lord.**

holiness, underscored by the divine command, "tell them: Be holy, for I the LORD your God am holy" (Lev. 19:2). Detailing laws on sacrificial offerings, priesthood, and purity for individuals, the cultural community, and priests, Leviticus is thorough in guiding Israel on their spiritual journey. It also outlines the celebrations of eight national feasts. These regulations, though complex, illustrate God's deep desire for a close relationship with humanity, all pointing toward the ultimate sacrificial offering of Jesus Christ on the cross to redeem humankind, making them acceptable and compatible with a holy Creator. This system, designed by God, acts as both a way to establish a covenant

*A Popular Verse:* **Leviticus 19:2, "Speak to the whole congregation of Israel and tell them: Be holy because I, the Lord your God, am holy.**

relationship with Him and a mirror to show how far humans fall short of His holiness, as explained in Romans 3:19-23 and 7:7. Leviticus underscores the core theme of holiness, necessary for sinful people to engage with a holy God. Through animal sacrifices and obedience to God's word, the Hebrews achieved a form of "temporary holiness." This divine arrangement highlights not an obligation but God's profound desire for closeness with His creations, illustrating His willingness to bridge the gap between His nature and human sinfulness for the sake of communion.

**Personal Notes:**

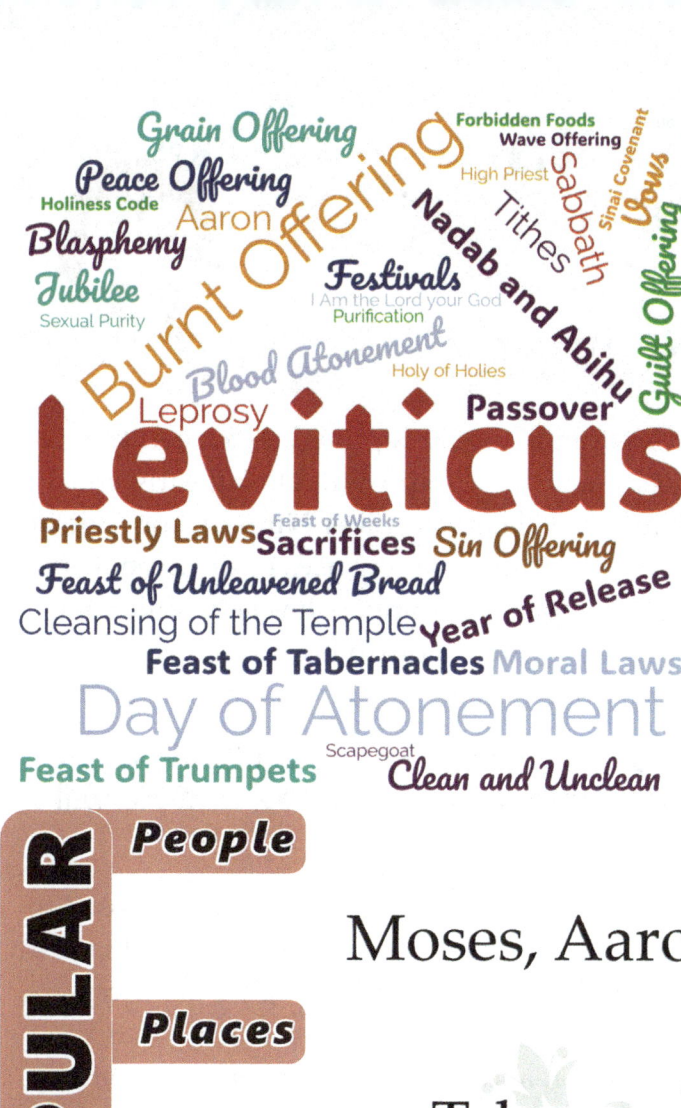

# Reflections on Leviticus
*Law and Holiness*

God, a sanctum of holiness, calls for the same sanctity from His children. While His people frequently fall short of these high standards, God, in His mercy, established temporary atonement through the sacrificial system. In response to His benevolence, God urges His people to embody holiness in every facet of life. By offering blessings as an incentive and warning of judgment, He gently prompts His people to repent and recommit to a steadfast devotion to Him.

## NOTABLE & POPULAR

**People**

Moses, Aaron, Nadab and Abihu

**Places**

Tabernacle, the Wilderness

**Events**

Establishment of priestly laws, Day of Atonement

**Verses**

**Leviticus 1:4** He is to lay his hand on the head of the burnt offering, so it can be accepted on his behalf to make atonement for him.

**Leviticus 17:11** For the life of the flesh is in the blood, and I have given it to you to make atonement for your souls upon the altar; for it is the blood that makes atonement for the soul.

**Leviticus 20:7** Consecrate yourselves, therefore, and be holy, because I am the Lord your God.

**Leviticus 26:3-4** If you follow My statutes and carefully keep My commandments, I will give you rains in their season, and the land will yield its produce, and the trees of the field will bear their fruit.

# NUMBERS

**Author:** Moses

**Time Written:** Between 1440 and 1400 B.C.

**Time Covered:** Around 1445 to 1407 B.C.

The title "Numbers" is derived from the Greek term "Arithmoi" in the Septuagint (the earliest translation of the Old Testament from Hebrew to Greek), which the Latin Vulgate (an early and important 5th century version of the Holy Bible, in Latin) translated as "Liber Numeri," or "Book of Numbers." These names reflect the book's content, specifically the two censuses of the Israelites conducted at Mount Sinai and on the plains of Moab. Additionally, Numbers has been called the "Book of the Journeyings," the "Book of the Murmurings," and the "Fourth Book of Moses," highlighting various aspects of its narrative. The majority of Numbers documents the often difficult

**A Key Verse:** Numbers 14:8, If the Lord delights in us, He will bring us into this land, a land flowing with milk and honey, and He will give it to us.

experiences of the Israelites as they wander in the wilderness, transforming what was supposed to be an eleven-day journey into a forty-year ordeal. Numbers not only recounts these events but also imparts crucial lessons about enduring times of hardship. It suggests that although wilderness periods are sometimes necessary, they are not meant to be permanent. The book teaches that prolonged trials may be used by God to capture our attention and alter our mindset or behaviors. Recognizing issues through self-reflection is only the first step; the key is to change our reaction towards God by embracing obedience. This can allow these challenging wilderness experiences to

**A Popular Verse:** Numbers 6:24-25, 'May the Lord bless you and keep you; may the Lord cause His face to shine upon you and be gracious to you;

reveal and refine our character, bringing us closer to God, enhancing our maturity as His children, and enabling us to better mirror His love to those around us. This transformational journey showcased in Numbers reveals that our choices have direct consequences, often severe. For example, when the initial generation of Israelites who left Egypt chose to rebel against God and sin against His commands, they were condemned to wander the wilderness for years—years which could have been spent in the Promised Land had they remained obedient. This stark lesson underlines the theme of the book: the profound impact of our decisions, particularly in relation to our obedience to God.

**Personal Notes:**

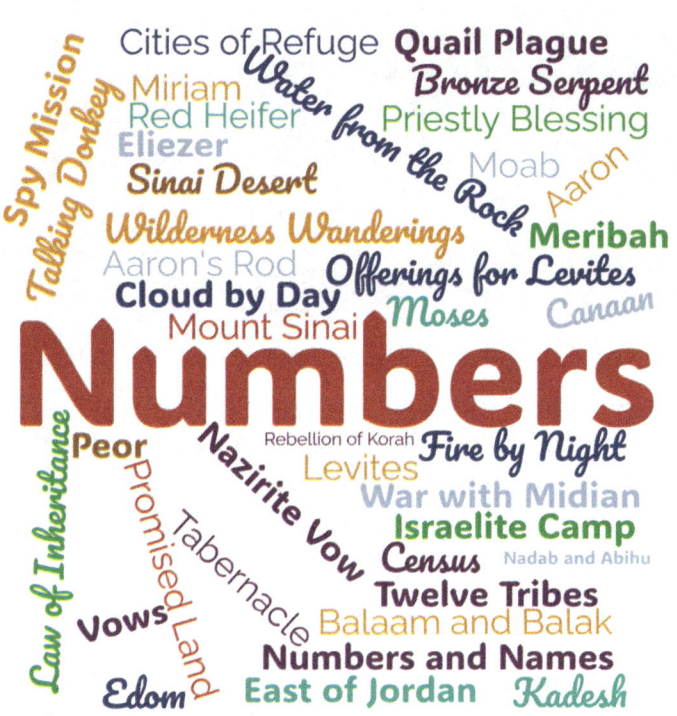

## Reflections on Numbers
*Wilderness Wanderings*

In His boundless wisdom, God prepared His people for service and the eventual triumph in taking the Promised Land. However, the first generation fell short, their success hindered by a lack of gratitude for God's generosity and fear of the Canaanites' strength. Yet, ever patient and persistent, the Lord nurtured a new generation for the journey ahead, emphasizing that their victory depended on their unwavering faithfulness to Him.

## NOTABLE & POPULAR

**People**

Moses, Aaron, Joshua, Caleb, Balaam

**Places**

Wilderness of Paran, Plains of Moab

**Events**

Census, Spies in Canaan, Korah's Rebellion, Balaam's Prophecies

**Verses**

**Numbers 12:6-8a** He said, "Hear now My words: If there is a prophet among you, I, the Lord, will reveal Myself to him in a vision; I will speak to him in a dream. But this is not so with My servant Moses; he is faithful in all My house. I speak with him face to face, clearly and not in riddles; he sees the form of the Lord….

**Numbers 14:30-34** Surely none of you will enter the land in which I swore to settle you, except Caleb son of Jephunneh and Joshua son of Nun. But I will bring your children, whom you said would become plunder, into the land you have rejected—and they will enjoy it. As for you, however, your bodies will fall in this wilderness. Your children will be shepherds in the wilderness for forty years, and they will suffer for your unfaithfulness until the last of your bodies lies in the wilderness. In keeping with the forty days you spied out the land, you shall bear your guilt forty years—a year for each day—and you will experience My alienation.

# DEUTERONOMY

**Author:** Moses

**Time Written:** Around 1406 B.C.

**Time Covered:** Around 1407 to 1406 B.C.

Deuteronomy, often referred to as Moses' "Upper Desert Discourse," presents a series of parting speeches by the venerable 120-year-old leader to the new generation set to enter the Promised Land of Canaan (modern day Israel). Deuteronomy completes the five books - known collectively as the Pentateuch in Greek and as the Torah to Jews - all authored by The Hebrew prophet, teacher, and administrator who had endured the arduous forty-year trek through the wilderness. The Jewish tradition calls Deuteronomy Mishneh Hattorah, meaning "Repetition of the Law," while the Greek Septuagint (the earliest translation of the Old Testament from Hebrew to Greek) termed it "To

**A Key Verse:** Deuteronomy 4:2, You must not add to or subtract from what I command you, so that you may keep the commandments of the Lord your God that I am giving you.

Deuteronomion Touto," or "This Second Law," from which the English title "Deuteronomy" derives. But, Deuteronomy is not a new law but rather a reiteration and expansion of the original laws given at Mount Sinai. Deuteronomy begins by recapping Israel's forty-year journey in the wilderness—a narrative Moses uses to emphasize the crucial lessons of obedience to God and the dire consequences of disobedience that prevented an entire generation from entering the promised land. Unlike Leviticus, which focuses on priestly duties, Deuteronomy is more concerned with the layperson's obligations and responsibilities. Moses uses this opportunity to remind the new

**A Popular Verse:** Deut. 6:4-5, Hear, O Israel: The Lord our God, the Lord is One. And you shall love the Lord your God with all your heart and with all your soul and with all your strength.

generation of the reasons their predecessors perished in the wilderness, highlighting the consequences of ignoring God's commands. The overarching theme of Deuteronomy is encapsulated in one pivotal command: "remember." Often called the "Book of Remembrance," it urges the faithful to keep alive the memory of their journey with God—the victories and defeats, and the mundane alongside the miraculous. It teaches that remembrance is key, not only of God's past blessings but also of His laws and principles that govern life on earth. God, Deuteronomy teaches, is ever-present, offering encouragement, strength, and blessings, guiding His people through both trials and times of change.

**Personal Notes:**

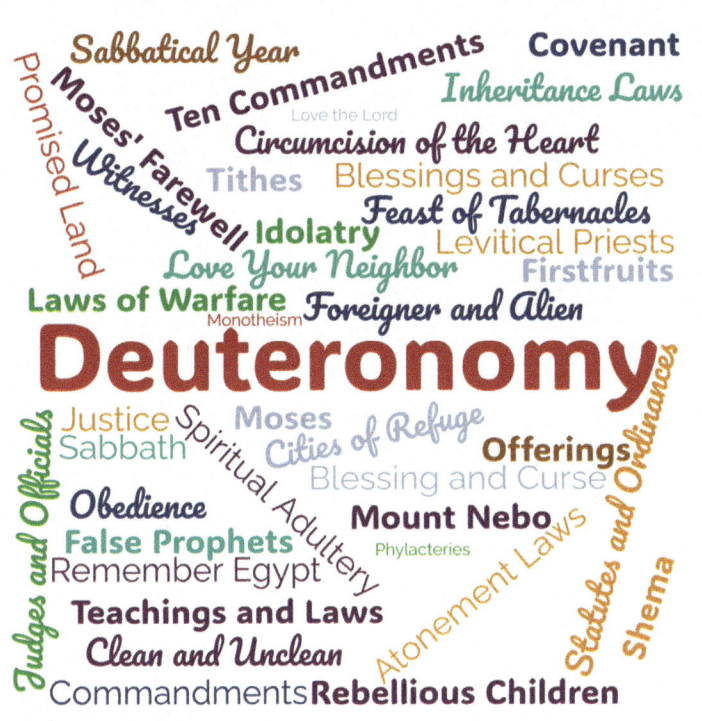

# Reflections on Deuteronomy
*Covenant Renewal*

As they stood on the plains of Moab, the Israelites were poised to absorb crucial lessons on covenant fidelity from their forebears. Guided by Moses' laws, they prepared to enter the Promised Land under Joshua's leadership. Obedience would bring blessings, while disobedience would result in curses. Their mission was to consistently renew their commitment to the covenant, both in Moab and as they stepped into their new homeland.

## People
Moses, Joshua

## Places
Moab, Mount Nebo

## Events
Moses' Farewell Speech, Renewal of the Covenant, Death of Moses

## Verses

**Deuteronomy 1:17** Show no partiality in judging; hear both small and great alike. Do not be intimidated by anyone, for judgment belongs to God. And bring to me any case too difficult for you, and I will hear it."

**Deuteronomy 6:6-7** These words I am commanding you today are to be upon your hearts. And you shall teach them diligently to your children and speak of them when you sit at home and when you walk along the road, when you lie down and when you get up.

**Deuteronomy 32:46-47** he said to them, "Take to heart all these words I testify among you today, so that you may command your children to carefully follow all the words of this law. For they are not idle words to you, because they are your life, and by them you will live long in the land that you are crossing the Jordan to possess."

# HISTORY

## Historic Books

Judges, 2-Kings, 1-Kings, 1-Chronicles, Ruth, Ezra, 2-Samuel, Joshua, 1-Samuel, Nehemiah, 2-Chronicles, Esther

The historical books of the Bible detail the era following Moses' death up to approximately 400 years before the birth of Christ. After Moses passed away, Joshua led the Israelites into the Promised Land, obeying God's command to defeat the nations residing there to avoid being corrupted by their sinfulness. However, Israel failed to fully conquer these peoples. Following Joshua's death, a series of judges governed Israel during a time marked by significant moral decline. Eventually, the Israelites demanded a king, rejecting God's leadership in favor of a human ruler, a decision that did not prove wise.

Saul became Israel's first king but failed to remain faithful to God, leading to his replacement by David, a man known for his deep devotion to God's heart. After David's death, his son Solomon ascended the throne. God blessed Solomon with unparalleled wisdom and immense wealth, and he built the first temple, gaining great fame. However, in his later years, Solomon's heart turned to other gods, influenced by his many wives. This disobedience led to the kingdom's division into the northern kingdom of Israel and the southern kingdom of Judah. Most of the subsequent kings were unfaithful to God, leading to the downfall of both kingdoms, with Judah being exiled to Babylon.

After 70 years in Babylon, a remnant of Jews returned to the Promised Land. These historical records serve as a poignant reminder of Israel's continual struggle with faithfulness and the consequences of turning away from God. They underscore the importance of steadfast devotion and the repercussions of disobedience, echoing the persistent call for holiness and faithfulness to God's covenant.

**Personal Notes:**

# JOSHUA

**Author:** Most Likely: Joshua

**Time Written:** Between 1400 and 1370 B.C.

**Time Covered:** Around 1406 to 1375 B.C.

Joshua, the inaugural book of the twelve historical books ranging from Joshua to Esther, serves as a crucial bridge from the era of Moses to the unfolding of Israel's national history. Under the skilled leadership of Joshua, Israel engages in three significant military campaigns against numerous enemy armies, learning that true victory relies on faith in God and adherence to His commands rather than on military prowess or sheer numbers. Spanning approximately fifty years, the narrative of Joshua describes Israel's transformation from a disjointed group of refugees into a unified nation of twelve tribes, jointly securing the land promised by God. This generation of Israelites, unlike

*A Key Verse:* Joshua 1:8, This Book of the Law must not depart from your mouth; meditate on it day and night, so that you may be careful to do everything written in it. For then you will prosper and succeed in all you do.

their predecessors, heeds God's directive to cross the Jordan River, motivated by God's assurance to Joshua (1:5): "As I was with Moses, so will I be with you; I will never leave you nor forsake you." This promise is dramatically affirmed as God miraculously enables them to enter the Promised Land over dry ground (Josh. 3). While the book of Joshua does not depict an uninterrupted series of triumphs, it candidly recounts both the victories and challenges encountered as the nation gradually takes possession of Canaan. By the conclusion of the book, an aged Joshua remains resolute in his faith, challenging the Israelites with a powerful declaration: "Choose for yourselves

*A Popular Verse:* Joshua 1:9, Have I not commanded you to be strong and courageous? Do not be afraid; do not be discouraged, for the Lord your God is with you wherever you go."

this day whom you will serve, whether the gods your fathers served beyond the Euphrates, or the gods of the Amorites, in whose land you are living. As for me and my house, we will serve the LORD!" (Josh. 24:15). The predominant theme of Joshua is the critical importance of heeding God's words to maintain fellowship with Him. God's instructions to Joshua to be courageous and trust in His guidance were pivotal, demonstrating that obedience to - and faith in - God alone, charts the path to historical significance and to both our personal and collective victories.

**Personal Notes:**

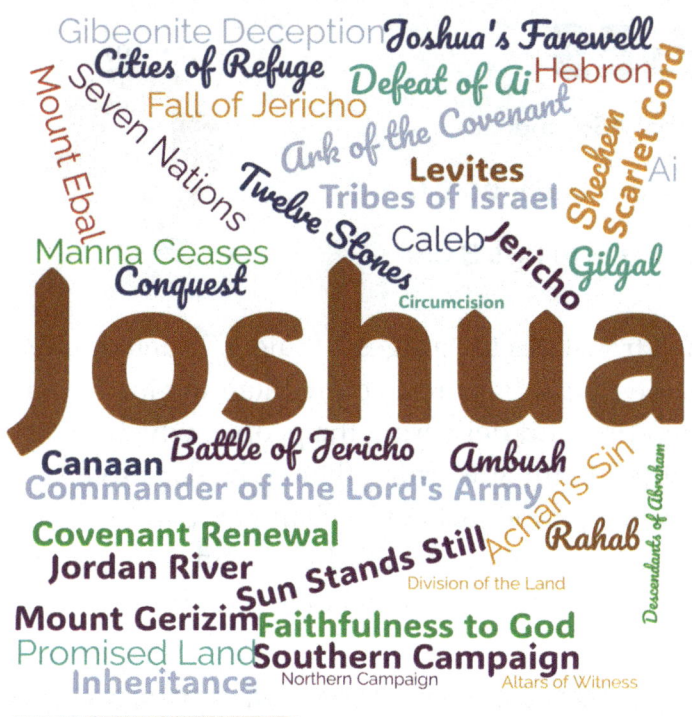

# Reflections on Joshua
*Conquest and Settlement*

Under Joshua's leadership, God granted Israel numerous triumphs in the Promised Land, though many challenges still lay ahead. As God's appointed leader, Joshua played a crucial role in dividing the land and determining its future stewardship. His period of covenant renewal established a model, providing a blueprint for future generations to reinvigorate their faith.

## NOTABLE & POPULAR

**People**

Joshua, Rahab, Achan

**Places**

Jericho, Ai, Gibeon

**Events**

Crossing of Jordan, Fall of Jericho, Sun Standing Still

**Verses**

**Joshua 1:7-8** Above all, be strong and very courageous. Be careful to observe all the law that My servant Moses commanded you. Do not turn from it to the right or to the left, so that you may prosper wherever you go. This Book of the Law must not depart from your mouth; meditate on it day and night, so that you may be careful to do everything written in it. For then you will prosper and succeed in all you do.

**Joshua 24:14-15** Now, therefore, fear the Lord and serve Him in sincerity and truth; cast aside the gods your fathers served beyond the Euphrates and in Egypt, and serve the Lord. But if it is unpleasing in your sight to serve the Lord, then choose for yourselves this day whom you will serve, whether the gods your fathers served beyond the Euphrates, or the gods of the Amorites in whose land you are living. As for me and my house, we will serve the Lord!"

# JUDGES

**Author:** Most Likely: Samuel

**Time Written:** Between 1045 and 1000 B.C.

**Time Covered:** Around 1375 to 1075 B.C.

The Hebrew title of the Book of Judges, "Shophetim," translates to "judges," "rulers," "deliverers," or "saviors." The term "Shophet" encompasses not only the judicial roles of maintaining justice and resolving disputes, but also the dynamic roles of liberating and delivering the people, which the judges fulfilled by first rescuing the Israelites and subsequently governing them. The narrative spans from the demise of Joshua, Moses' successor, to the period just before Saul's monarchy, capturing the era in which Israel was led by fourteen judges prior to establishing a kingship. Judges starkly contrasts with the Book of Joshua. Whereas Joshua depicts an obedient and faithful

**A Key Verse:** Judges 2:16, Then the Lord raised up judges, who saved them from the hands of those who plundered them.

populace under virtuous leadership conquering the land with God's aid, Judges presents a cycle of disobedience and idol worship, leading to recurrent defeat due to the Israelites' rebellion against God. Through seven of these recurring cycles, the book of Judges illustrates Israel's departure from God's laws in favor of subjective moral standpoints where "everyone did what was right in his own eyes" (Judges 21:25), eliciting internal corruption and external oppression. Over these three centuries, despite repeated falls into the "sin cycle" and a spiritual decline, God's mercy remained, as He raised up military leaders to liberate and guide the nation back to devout worship. Judges

**A Popular Verse:** Judges 21:25, In those days there was no king in Israel; everyone did what was right in his own eyes.

serves as a potent reminder of God's enduring mercy and grace—He is always ready to restore and bless His people upon their repentance. The book emphasizes that God's patience is vast, extending grace and mercy even when His people are caught in a chronic cycle of falling away, judgment, and repentance, affirming that obedience invariably attracts blessings.

**Personal Notes:**

# Reflections on Judges
*Cycles of Disobedience*

The tribes of Israel faltered in completely conquering the land, and their shortcomings led to inevitable consequences. God's interim remedy was to provide Judges, but their leadership yielded only fleeting blessings. Even the appointment of the Levites failed to offer lasting guidance. Indeed, what God's people truly needed was a righteous king, preferably from the tribe of Judah rather than Benjamin, to lead them effectively.

## Notable & Popular

**People**

Deborah, Gideon, Samson, Jephthah

**Places**

Jezreel Valley, Gibeah, Shiloh

**Events**

Cycles of Apostasy and Deliverance, Samson's Exploits

**Verses**

**Judges 2:17-19** Israel, however, did not listen to their judges. Instead, they prostituted themselves with other gods and bowed down to them. They quickly turned from the way of their fathers, who had walked in obedience to the Lord's commandments; they did not do as their fathers had done. Whenever the Lord raised up a judge for the Israelites, He was with that judge and saved them from the hands of their enemies while the judge was still alive; for the Lord was moved to pity by their groaning under those who oppressed them and afflicted them. But when the judge died, the Israelites became even more corrupt than their fathers, going after other gods to serve them and bow down to them. They would not give up their evil practices and stubborn ways.

**Judges 10:15** "We have sinned," the Israelites said to the Lord. "Deal with us as You see fit; but please deliver us today!"

# RUTH

**Author:** Possibly: Samuel

**Time Written:** Between 1011 and 931 B.C.

**Time Covered:** 1140 B.C.

Ruth is a poignant tale of love, devotion, and redemption, set against the tumultuous backdrop of the era of the Judges. It narrates the journey of Ruth, a Moabite woman who abandons her pagan roots to embrace the people and God of Israel. Her steadfast faithfulness during a period of widespread national disloyalty leads to divine rewards: a new husband named Boaz, a son named Obed, and a distinguished place in the lineage of Christ, becoming the great-grandmother of King David. The story begins with the tragedy that befalls Ruth and her mother-in-law, Naomi. After the deaths of their husbands, the pair faces a bleak future alone. When Naomi decides to return to her

*A Key Verse:* Ruth 4:14, Then the women said to Naomi, "Blessed be the Lord, who has not left you this day without a kinsman-redeemer. May his name become famous in Israel.

hometown of Bethlehem, Ruth demonstrates profound loyalty by choosing to accompany her, despite the challenges of living as a foreigner. She famously declares, "Your people will be my people, and your God will be my God" (Ruth 1:16). Upon arriving in Bethlehem, Ruth starts collecting leftover grain in the fields for subsistence, unknowingly working in the fields of Boaz, a wealthy relative of Naomi's late husband. Boaz notices Ruth's hard work and dedication and extends generous hospitality to her, offering protection and ample provision. Ruth's humble circumstances belie her significant role in God's plan. When Boaz praises her actions and seeks

*A Popular Verse:* Ruth 1:16, But Ruth replied: "Do not urge me to leave you or to turn from following you. For wherever you go, I will go, and wherever you live, I will live; your people will be my people, and your God will be my God.

God's blessing for her, he unknowingly steps into his divine role as Ruth's Kinsman-Redeemer (a male relative who, according to Old Testament law, had the right or responsibility to act on behalf of a relative who was in trouble or need). Through a series of providential events, Ruth and Boaz marry, ensuring the continuation of a lineage that would ultimately lead to Jesus Christ. The story of Ruth teaches the profound impact of placing trust in God with our circumstances and future. Through Ruth's life, we also gain insight into God's redemptive love, mirrored in Christ, our ultimate Kinsman-Redeemer. The narrative underscores a powerful theme: Faithfulness to God, even in an environment of unfaithfulness, invariably attracts divine blessings.

**Personal Notes:**

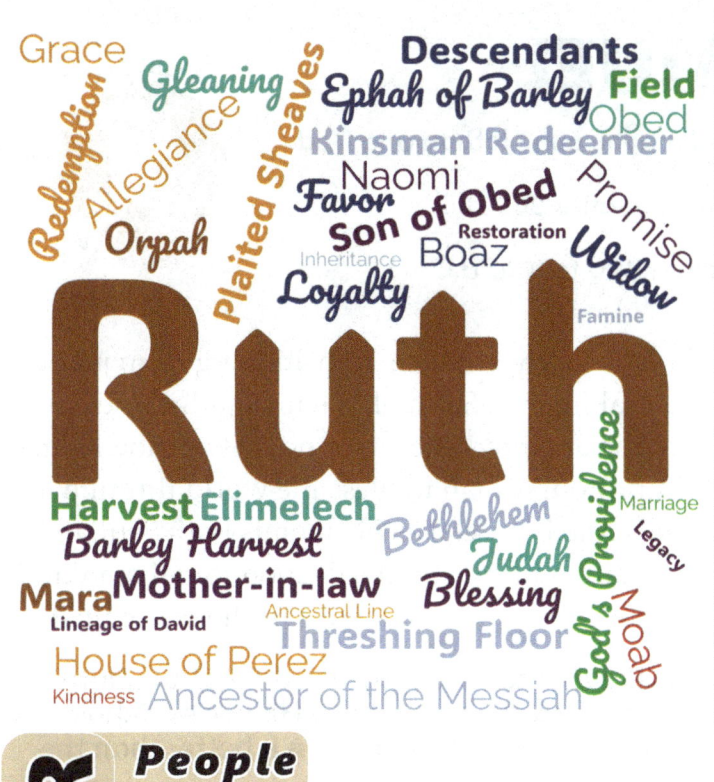

## Reflections on Ruth
*Loyalty and Redemption*

While God's providence may appear strict at times, it ultimately enhances blessings for His people. When love and devotion in families are grounded in God's law, they bring forth joy and happiness. Additionally, God honored David's lineage, as His chosen royal line, and thus fulfilled His promise in saying: "your throne will be established forever." God's promise was fulfilled through Jesus Christ, and Ruth was a part of that blessed family line.

## NOTABLE & POPULAR

**People**

Ruth, Naomi, Boaz

**Places**

Moab, Bethlehem

**Events**

Famine and Return, Ruth's Loyalty, Boaz as Kinsman-Redeemer

**Verses**

**Ruth 1:16** But Ruth replied: "Do not urge me to leave you or to turn from following you. For wherever you go, I will go, and wherever you live, I will live; your people will be my people, and your God will be my God.

**Ruth 3:9** "Who are you?" he asked. "I am your servant Ruth," she replied. "Spread the corner of your garment over me, for you are a kinsman-redeemer."

**Ruth 4:13** So Boaz took Ruth, and she became his wife. And when he had relations with her, the Lord enabled her to conceive, and she gave birth to a son.

**Ruth 4:17** The neighbor women said, "A son has been born to Naomi," and they named him Obed. He became the father of Jesse, the father of David.

# 1 SAMUEL

**Author:** Probably Samuel, and maybe also Nathan and Gad

**Time Written:** Sometime after 960 B.C.

**Time Covered:** Around 1100 to 1010 B.C

In the Book of 1 Samuel, we witness a pivotal shift in Israel's governance, transitioning from judges to royal leadership. The narrative introduces three central figures: Samuel, the final judge and premier prophet; Saul, the inaugural king; and David, the anointed successor not yet acknowledged by Saul. This book highlights the ushering in of God's profound plan to bless the world through a faithful king, setting the stage for the Messiah. Samuel's role is crucial as he anoints both Saul and David, marking a divine orchestration in leadership meant to bring about salvation for all mankind. Throughout these challenging times, David, though not yet king, demonstrates resilience against

**A Key Verse:** 1 Samuel 15:22, But Samuel declared: "Does the Lord delight in burnt offerings and sacrifices as much as in obedience to His voice? Behold, obedience is better than sacrifice, and attentiveness is better than the fat of rams.

great adversities. God's protection over David underscores His unwavering commitment to His plans, ensuring David's vital role in the history of Israel and the unfolding of divine salvation. This illustrates a central theme in 1 Samuel: God's sovereignty and faithfulness, triumphing even amid human error and sin. Initially recognized as the "Book of Samuel" the originally unified text was divided in the Septuagint (the earliest translation of the Old Testament from Hebrew to Greek), for convenience sake, into two parts: 1 Samuel and 2 Samuel. But though two books instead of one, this book begins the telling of a cohesive story of God's guidance under the dynamics of changing

**A Popular Verse:** 1 Samuel 16:7, But the Lord said to Samuel, "Do not consider his appearance or height, for I have rejected him; the Lord does not see as man does. For man sees the outward appearance, but the Lord sees the heart."

leadership. The Septuagint, followed by the Latin Vulgate (an early and important 5th century version of the Holy Bible, in Latin), named it under themes of kingship and kingdoms, reflecting the foundational shifts in Israel's governance. These titles and divisions, though varied, affirm the enduring message of God's ultimate authority and His faithful preservation of His chosen leaders. 1 Samuel is a narrative replete with assurance for today's believers that God fulfills His promises, guiding and empowering those He has called for His purposes.

**Personal Notes:**

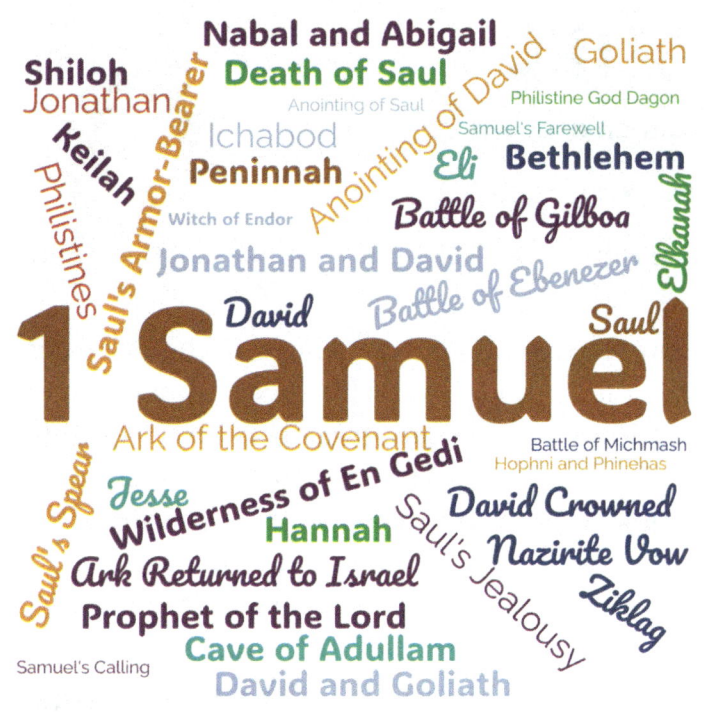

# Reflections on 1 Samuel
*Samuel, Saul, David*

God desired a king for His people, one of His own choosing. He carefully charted the course for His anointed ruler, designating David's house as the enduring royal lineage. Even as David's kingdom displayed moments of frailty, the beacon of hope for God's people continued to shine through his family.

## NOTABLE & POPULAR

**People**

Samuel, Saul, David, Jonathan

**Places**

Shiloh, Gibeah, Bethlehem, Philistia

**Events**

Anointing of Saul and David, David and Goliath

**Verses**

**1 Samuel 13:13-14** "You have acted foolishly," Samuel declared. "You have not kept the command that the Lord your God gave you; if you had, the Lord would have established your kingdom over Israel for all time. But now your kingdom will not endure; the Lord has sought a man after His own heart and appointed him ruler over His people, because you have not kept the command of the Lord."

**1 Samuel 15:22-23** But Samuel declared: "Does the Lord delight in burnt offerings and sacrifices as much as in obedience to His voice? Behold, obedience is better than sacrifice, and attentiveness is better than the fat of rams. For rebellion is like the sin of divination, and arrogance is like the wickedness of idolatry. Because you have rejected the word of the Lord, He has rejected you as king."

# 2 SAMUEL

**Author:** Possibly Nathan and Gad

**Time Written:** Sometime after 960 B.C.

**Time Covered:** Around 1010 to 970 B.C.

After enduring years of preparation and numerous battles, David finally ascended to the throne as the king of Israel, marking a significant fulfillment of God's promises. The Book of 2 Samuel offers a detailed account of David's reign, capturing both his triumphs and trials. Initially ruling over Judah and eventually uniting and leading the entire nation of Israel, David's journey from shepherd to king is one of the most compelling narratives in the Bible. Despite the grievous sins of adultery and murder, and the ensuing turmoil within his own family and his kingdom, David remains a poignant example of a flawed yet deeply devoted servant of God. David's life, as depicted in

**A Key Verse:** 2 Samuel 7:16, Your house and kingdom will endure forever before Me, and your throne will be established forever."

2 Samuel illustrates the complexities of his character. David's story is not just about his notable successes but also his profound lows of falling into sin, seeking repentance, and ultimately being restored by God. He is both warrior and worshiper. And not only is he contemplative in his sin but very remorseful and penitent in his confession of such. David's spiritual resilience shines through as he consistently seeks to deepen his relationship with the Lord, spending precious moments in solitude with God. This commitment to seeking God's presence laid the foundation for his spiritual greatness. 2 Samuel teaches us that God does not seek perfection in His servants, but rather a heart

**A Popular Verse:** 2 Samuel 7:22, How great You are, O Lord GOD! For there is none like You, and there is no God but You, according to everything we have heard with our own ears.

devoted to loving and serving Him despite human flaws and failures. It shows that while sin has its inevitable consequences, God's forgiveness and redemption are always within reach for those who return to Him with a repentant heart. Through David's life, we learn about God's sovereignty, His perfect timing, and His ability to use imperfect people to fulfill His divine purposes. This narrative reassures us that our mistakes don't define us when our hearts are tuned to God's will and purposes.

**Personal Notes:**

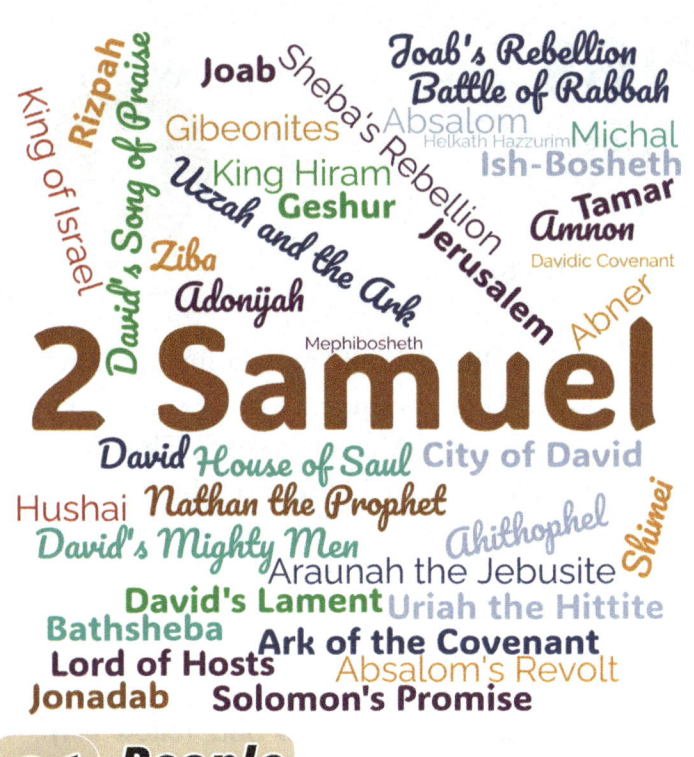

# Reflections on 2 Samuel
*David's Reign*

God's design for His people included a monarch of His choosing. He skillfully prepared the path for His anointed king, selecting David's house as the everlasting royal dynasty. Despite the weaknesses that appeared during David's reign, his lineage remained a beacon of hope for God's people.

## NOTABLE & POPULAR

**People**

David, Bathsheba, Absalom, Nathan, Joab

**Places**

Jerusalem, Hebron, Ammon

**Events**

David's Reign, Bathsheba Incident, Absalom's Rebellion

**Verses**

2 Samuel 5:10 And David became greater and greater, for the Lord God of Hosts was with him.

2 Samuel 19:4 But the king covered his face and cried out at the top of his voice, "O my son Absalom! O Absalom, my son, my son!"

2 Samuel 22:2-4 He said: "The Lord is my rock, my fortress, and my deliverer. My God is my rock, in whom I take refuge, my shield, and the horn of my salvation. My stronghold, my refuge, and my Savior, You save me from violence. I will call upon the Lord, who is worthy to be praised; so shall I be saved from my enemies.

2 Samuel 22:31 As for God, His way is perfect; the word of the Lord is flawless. He is a shield to all who take refuge in Him.

# 1 KINGS

**Author:** Possibly Jeremiah

**Time Written:** Likely between 560 and 540 B.C.

**Time Covered:** Around 970 to 853 B.C.

Originally, the books of Kings were a single text in the Hebrew Bible, titled "Melechim," meaning "Kings." However, the Septuagint, translating the text into Greek and requiring more scroll space due to the language difference, divided the narrative in the middle of Ahaziah's story. This division resulted in what the Septuagint called the "Third and Fourth Kingdoms," following the "First and Second Kingdoms" designation it assigned to what are commonly known as the books of Samuel. The narrative of 1 Kings begins by detailing the reign of Solomon, under whom Israel reached unprecedented heights of power, prosperity, and splendor. Solomon's reign marked the zenith of

*A Key Verse:* 1 Kings 18:21, Then Elijah approached all the people and said, "How long will you waver between two opinions? If the Lord is God, follow Him. But if Baal is God, follow him." But the people did not answer a word.

Israel's history, epitomized by his crowning achievement—the construction of the Temple in Jerusalem, which earned the nation immense respect and admiration globally. Yet, the latter years of Solomon's reign were marred by his waning commitment to God, a consequence of his being influenced by his pagan wives. This ultimately led to his heart being divided—and consequently the division of his kingdom. The Book of 1 Kings continues to recount the subsequent era, illustrating the decline of a nation split in two, with leaders who frequently ignored divine guidance resulting in a spiritual despair that spilled over onto the people. This theme of fidelity to

*A Popular Verse:* 1 Kings 3:9, Therefore give Your servant an understanding heart to judge Your people and to discern between good and evil. For who is able to govern this great people of Yours?"

God underscores the book, suggesting that steadfast devotion to God is paramount for both individuals and nations. As long as Solomon and the people remained devout, they thrived. But their deviation from faith led to internal strife and external conquest, culminating in the Kingdom's downfall and the exile of its people, a poignant reminder of the critical importance of unwavering faithfulness to God.

**Personal Notes:**

# Reflections on 1 Kings
*Solomon and Division*

The exile of Israel and Judah, harsh as it was, stood justified given the nation's repeated and profound acts of apostasy. Despite the shortcomings of David's descendants, God's promises to his lineage held steadfast. God called His exiled people to repentance for their transgressions. The promise of a magnificent restoration awaited Israel, dependent upon their readiness to repent.

## NOTABLE & POPULAR

**People**

Solomon, Elijah, Ahab, Jezebel

**Places**

Jerusalem, Samaria, Mount Carmel

**Events**

Solomon's Reign, Temple Construction, Division of Kingdom

**Verses**

**1 Kings 9:3** And the Lord said to him: "I have heard your prayer and petition before Me. I have consecrated this temple you have built by putting My Name there forever; My eyes and My heart will be there for all time.

**1 Kings 12:16** When all Israel saw that the king had refused to listen to them, they answered the king: "What portion do we have in David, and what inheritance in the son of Jesse? To your tents, O Israel! Look now to your own house, O David!" So the Israelites went home,

**1 Kings 12:28** After seeking advice, the king made two golden calves and said to the people, "Going up to Jerusalem is too much for you. Here, O Israel, are your gods, who brought you up out of the land of Egypt."

33

# 2 KINGS

**Author:** Possibly Jeremiah

**Time Written:** Likely between 560 and 540 B.C.

**Time Covered:** Around 852 to 586 B.C.

The Book of 2 Kings extends the tragic narrative started in 1 Kings, detailing the demise of two nations, Israel and Judah, as they spiral towards inevitable captivity. This account meticulously contrasts the rulers of both kingdoms, analyzing their reigns sequentially to provide a comprehensive overview. While Israel suffers under the rule of nineteen successive malevolent kings, leading to its fall to Assyria, Judah experiences fleeting moments of reform through a few righteous kings, though it too ultimately succumbs to sin and is led into Babylonian exile. Amidst this backdrop of decline, the figure of Elisha, Elijah's prophetic successor, stands out. Where Elijah's

*A Key Verse:* 2 Kings 17:13, Yet through all His prophets and seers, the Lord warned Israel and Judah, saying, "Turn from your wicked ways and keep My commandments and statutes, according to the entire Law that I commanded your fathers and delivered to you through My servants...

ministry was marked by powerful oratory, Elisha's was distinguished by his miraculous deeds. These include dividing the Jordan River, reviving a child, purifying poisoned stew, miraculously feeding multitudes, healing a leper, and even cursing a deceitful servant with leprosy. Elisha's miracles demonstrated his unique calling and God's powerful presence in a time of widespread faithlessness. Particularly poignant is his role in the anointing of Jehu, which would alter the course of Israel's monarchy. 2 Kings underscores sobering themes: the principle of sowing and reaping is evident as generations of disobedience lead Israel and Judah to ruin, highlighting the consequences

*A Popular Verse:* 2 Kings 2:11, As they were walking along and talking together, suddenly a chariot of fire with horses of fire appeared and separated the two of them, and Elijah went up into heaven in a whirlwind.

of turning away from God. Yet, there is also a message of hope through Elisha's extraordinary life, showing what can be achieved when one earnestly seeks God's empowerment. The plea for a double portion of God's spirit and the subsequent impact of Elisha's ministry reflect the potential for divine work through human obedience, even in the darkest times.

**Personal Notes:**

# Reflections on 2 Kings
*Exile of Israel*

The books of 1 and 2 Kings were originally one book whose author is not identified. Indications are that he was a compiler of historical sources who worked during the Babylonian exile. For the Reflection on Second Kings, see the Reflection on First Kings (one page back).

## NOTABLE & POPULAR

**People**

Elijah, Elisha, Hezekiah, Josiah

**Places**

Samaria, Jerusalem, Babylon

**Events**

Elijah and Elisha's Miracles, Fall of Samaria, Fall of Jerusalem

**Verses**

**2 Kings 8:19** Yet for the sake of His servant David, the Lord was unwilling to destroy Judah, since He had promised to maintain a lamp for David and his descendants forever.

**2 Kings 17:7-8** All this happened because the people of Israel had sinned against the Lord their God, who had brought them out of the land of Egypt from under the hand of Pharaoh king of Egypt. They had worshiped other gods and walked in the customs of the nations that the Lord had driven out before the Israelites, as well as in the practices introduced by the kings of Israel.

**2 Kings 24:2** And the Lord sent Chaldean, Aramean, Moabite, and Ammonite raiders against Jehoiakim in order to destroy Judah, according to the word that the Lord had spoken through His servants the prophets.

# 1 CHRONICLES

**Author:** Probably Ezra

**Time Written:** Likely between 450 and 425 B.C.

**Time Covered:** Around 1003 to 970 B.C.

The works known as 1 and 2 Chronicles were originally a single unified text in the Hebrew Bible. In the third century B.C., the Septuagint (an early and important 5th century version of the Holy Bible, in Latin) split this work into two parts, naming it "Of Things Omitted" to indicate its focus on events not detailed in the books of Samuel and Kings. Later, Jerome, in creating the Latin Vulgate (an early and important 5th century version of the Holy Bible, in Latin), coined the term "Chronicles" intending it to encompass the "Chronicles of the Whole of Sacred History." While covering the same historical period as 2 Samuel through 2 Kings, 1 and 2 Chronicles approach the

*A Key Verse:* 1 Chronicles 29:1, Yours, O Lord, is the greatness and the power and the glory and the splendor and the majesty, for everything in heaven and on earth belongs to You. Yours, O Lord, is the kingdom, and You are exalted as head over all.

narrative from a distinctly different angle. These books do not simply reiterate the contents of the earlier texts; instead, they offer a 'divine commentary' on the history of God's people, focusing particularly on the House of David's kingdom of Judah from a religious standpoint. For example, these books delve deeply into the construction of the Temple and the intricacies of Israelite worship, offering a priestly and spiritual interpretation rather than the more political and moral perspectives seen in Samuel and Kings. The Book of 1 Chronicles starts with the genealogy of David, setting the stage for a detailed examination of his righteous rule and the spiritual implications of his

*A Popular Verse:* 1 Chronicles 4:10, And Jabez called out to the God of Israel, "If only You would bless me and enlarge my territory! May Your hand be with me and keep me from harm, so that I will be free from pain." And God granted the request of Jabez.

leadership. Central themes highlighted include the importance of correct worship of the true and living God, as exemplified by David, and the overarching sovereignty of God throughout the history of His people. This perspective underscores the Chronicles' intent to portray a history where divine and human actions interweave through the lens of worship and piety.

**Personal Notes:**

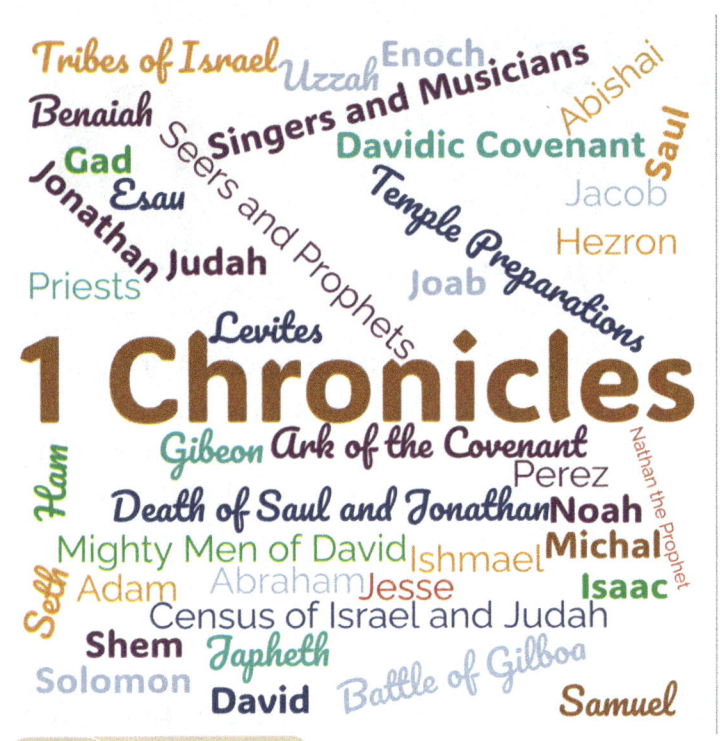

# Reflections on 1 Chronicles
*David's Legacy*

The united kingdoms of David and Solomon stand as benchmarks for God's people in their quest for divine blessings. Each generation of Israelites was influenced by its adherence to God's guidelines for kingship, the Temple, and the unity of His people. Israel's historical narrative delivers valuable insights, teaching future generations about the faithfulness and priorities that God expects from them.

## NOTABLE & POPULAR

**People**

David, Solomon

**Places**

Jerusalem

**Events**

Genealogies, Davidic Covenant, Preparations for Temple

**Verses**

**1 Chronicles 11:1-2** Then all Israel came together to David at Hebron and said, "Here we are, your own flesh and blood. Even in times past, while Saul was king, you were the one who led Israel out and brought them back. And the Lord your God said, 'You will shepherd My people Israel, and you will be ruler over them.'"

**1 Chronicles 21:13** David answered Gad, "I am deeply distressed. Please, let me fall into the hand of the Lord, for His mercies are very great; but do not let me fall into the hands of men."

**1 Chronicles 29:11** Yours, O Lord, is the greatness and the power and the glory and the splendor and the majesty, for everything in heaven and on earth belongs to You. Yours, O Lord, is the kingdom, and You are exalted as head over all.

# 2 CHRONICLES

**Author:** Probably Ezra

**Time Written:** Likely between 450 and 425 B.C.

**Time Covered:** Around 967 to 609 B.C.

History
Books 6 - 12

Second Chronicles, continuing the narrative from 1 Chronicles, aligns with the accounts of 1 and 2 Kings but primarily excludes the northern kingdom of Israel, focusing instead on Judah due to Israel's adoption of false worship practices and its non-recognition of the Temple in Jerusalem. This book chronicles the decline of a nation increasingly distancing itself from God, highlighting the severe consequences of this apostasy. It emphasizes the narratives of kings who emulated the devout leadership style of King David and spotlights five reformist kings—Asa, Jehoshaphat, Joash, Hezekiah, and Josiah—who endeavored to purge the nation of idolatry and restore proper worship

*A Key Verse:* 2 Chronicles 2:1, Now Solomon purposed to build a house for the Name of the Lord and a royal palace for himself.

practices. Central to the narrative of 2 Chronicles is the Temple and its associated rituals, underscoring the idea that proper worship of God was essential for the nation's survival. The book opens with the construction of Solomon's magnificent temple and concludes with King Cyrus's decree that permits the Jews to return and reconstruct their temple after more than four centuries. Throughout 2 Chronicles, themes of temple worship and the cyclic pattern of apostasy and revival are prominent, illustrating the tragic yet redemptive history of a people who frequently diverged from, yet periodically returned to, their foundational spiritual commitments. The enduring message

*A Popular Verse:* 2 Chronicles 7:14, and if My people who are called by My name humble themselves and pray and seek My face and turn from their wicked ways, then I will hear from heaven, forgive their sin, and heal their land.

of 2 Chronicles is that, despite human rebellion, God remains steadfast in achieving His divine purposes for humanity.

**Personal Notes:**

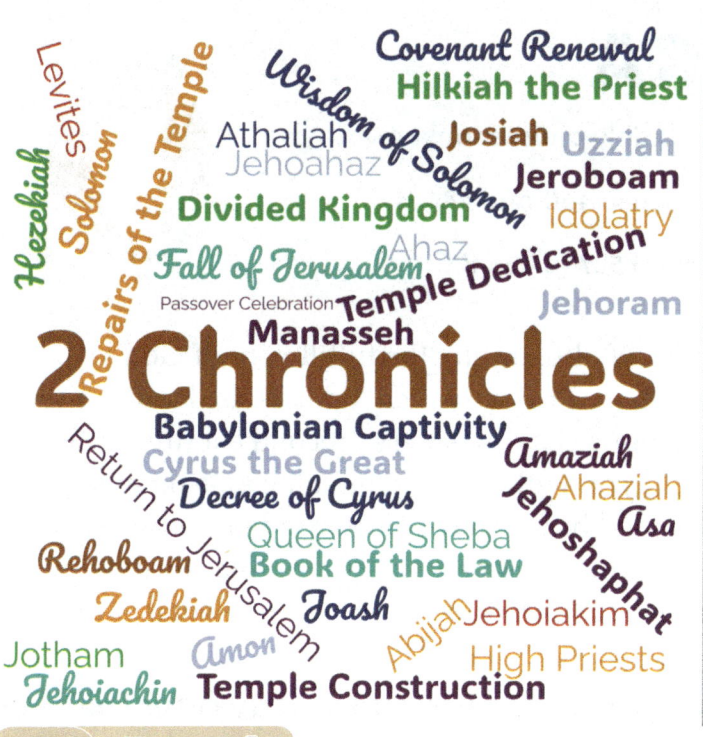

# Reflections on 2 Chronicles
*Judah's History*

The books of 1 and 2 Chronicles were originally one book whose author is not identified. Early Jewish tradition says that Ezra wrote Chronicles. But because that is uncertain, many people refer to the author as simply, "The Chronicler." For the Reflection on Second Chronicles, see the Reflection on First Chronicles (one page back).

## NOTABLE & POPULAR

**People**

Solomon, Rehoboam, Hezekiah, Josiah

**Places**

Jerusalem, Temple

**Events**

History of Judah, Solomon's Reign, Revival under Hezekiah and Josiah

**Verses**

**2 Chronicles 29:1-2** Hezekiah was twenty-five years old when he became king, and he reigned in Jerusalem twenty-nine years. His mother's name was Abijah, the daughter of Zechariah. And he did what was right in the eyes of the Lord, just as his father David had done.

**2 Chronicles 36:14** Furthermore, all the leaders of the priests and the people multiplied their unfaithful deeds, following all the abominations of the nations, and they defiled the house of the Lord, which He had consecrated in Jerusalem.

**2 Chronicles 36:23** "This is what Cyrus king of Persia says: 'The Lord, the God of heaven, who has given me all the kingdoms of the earth, has appointed me to build a house for Him at Jerusalem in Judah. Whoever among you belongs to His people, may the Lord his God be with him, and may he go up.'"

# EZRA

**Author:** Likely Ezra with possibly another unknown

**Time Written:** Likely between 460 and 440 B.C.

**Time Covered:** Around 537 to 456 B.C.

The Book of Ezra picks up where 2 Chronicles leaves off, illustrating the fulfillment of God's promise to return His people to the Promised Land (then Canaan, which today is the land of Israel) after a seventy-year exile. This return from Babylon, often seen as Israel's "second exodus," was modest compared to the monumental exodus from Egypt, with only a remnant choosing to leave Babylon. Ezra details two significant returns: the first led by Zerubbabel, focused on reconstructing the temple (chapters 1-6), and the second led by Ezra himself, aimed at restoring the spiritual life of the people (chapters 7-10). Spanning these two events is an interlude of nearly sixty years, during

**A Key Verse:** Ezra 9:10, And now, our God, what can we say after this? For we have forsaken the commandments

which time Esther becomes queen of Persia (see Book of Esther). Ezra's narrative is a testament to redemption and divine faithfulness, emphasizing reliance on God's Word under all conditions. Highlighting this, Ezra reflects on prophecy made 150 years prior by Isaiah (Is. 44:28-45:7), which foretold the rise of Cyrus of Persia, and prophecies of Jeremiah (Jer. 25:11-12, 29:10) which foretold of how Cyrus would ultimately free the Jews from captivity. Following his conquest of Babylon, Cyrus issued a decree allowing the Jews to return to their homeland, reaffirming God's steadfast promise-keeping nature. Central to Ezra is the theme of the power and certainty of God's Word; the

**A Popular Verse:** Ezra 7:10, For Ezra had set his heart to study the Law of the Lord, to practice it, and to teach its statutes and ordinances in Israel.

events described are portrayed as direct fulfillments of prophetic declarations, specifically concerning God's promise through Jeremiah. This narrative reassures us of the truth that God's promises are dependable and reaffirms the enduring reliability of His Word, which remains relevant and faithful across millennia. If God has spoken it, we can trust it implicitly.

**Personal Notes:**

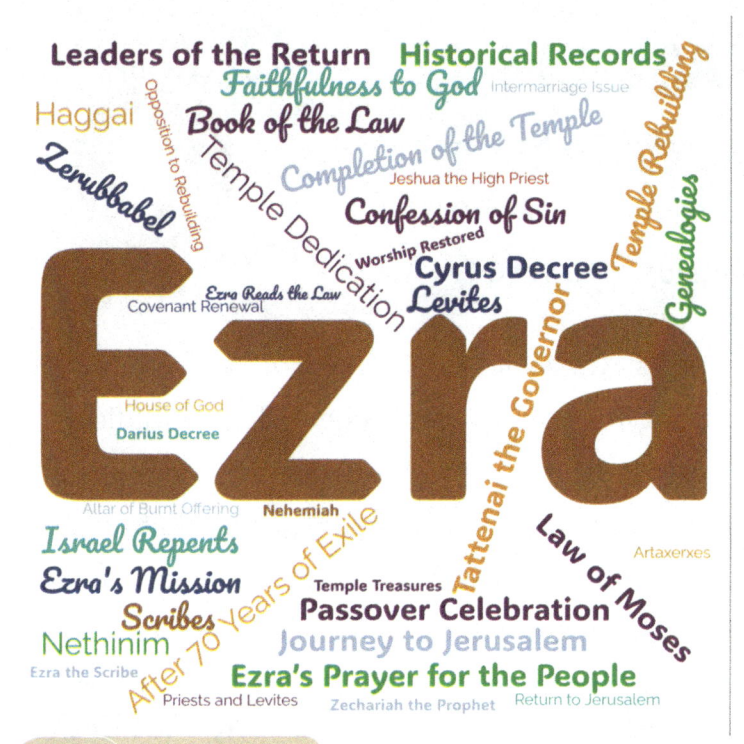

# Reflections on Ezra
*Return and Rebuilding*

God bestowed His favor and blessings on Zerubbabel, Ezra, and Nehemiah as they led the post-exilic restoration. In the midst of Israel's struggling revival, Ezra and Nehemiah emerged as bastions of faithful leadership. The Temple and Jerusalem served as pivotal centers, essential for directing God's blessings to His people. Repentance and holiness were the essential steps for God's people to receive His divine blessings.

## NOTABLE & POPULAR

**People**

Ezra, Zerubbabel

**Places**

Babylon, Jerusalem

**Events**

Return from Exile, Rebuilding the Temple

**Verses**

**Ezra 1:3** Whoever among you belongs to His people, may his God be with him, and may he go to Jerusalem in Judah and build the house of the Lord, the God of Israel; He is the God who is in Jerusalem.

**Ezra 3:11** And they sang responsively with praise and thanksgiving to the Lord: "For He is good; for His loving devotion to Israel endures forever." Then all the people gave a great shout of praise to the Lord, because the foundation of the house of the Lord had been laid.

**Ezra 7:6** this Ezra came up from Babylon. He was a scribe skilled in the Law of Moses, which the Lord, the God of Israel, had given. The king had granted Ezra all his requests, for the hand of the Lord his God was upon him.

# NEHEMIAH

**Author:** Possibly Ezra and Possibly Nehemiah

**Time Written:** Likely between 445 and 420 B.C.

**Time Covered:** Around 445 to 432 B.C.

The Book of Nehemiah, known in Hebrew as Nehemyah, translates to "Comfort of Yahweh," aptly named after its principal figure who is introduced right in the first verse. Nehemiah exemplifies exceptional leadership through his remarkable life as cup-bearer to King Artaxerxes of Persia. More than just a servant, Nehemiah was a confidant, adviser, and protector of the king, roles that demanded utmost loyalty and trust. Nehemiah's concern for Jerusalem, sparked by a report on the city's desolate condition, catapulted him into action. Learning that the city walls lay in ruins and the

*A Key Verse:* Nehemiah 6:3, So I sent messengers to them, saying, "I am doing a great work and cannot come down. Why should the work stop while I leave it to go down to you?"

citizens were disheartened, Nehemiah felt compelled to help rebuild not only the physical structures but also the spirit of the people. With the king's blessing to return to Jerusalem, he rallied his fellow countrymen to reconstruct the city's walls, a monumental task they completed in just fifty-two days despite internal disputes and external threats. This rapid construction was seen by many, including their adversaries, as a clear demonstration of divine intervention. However, the challenges Nehemiah faced extended beyond physical rebuilding; he also took on the spiritual and

*A Popular Verse:* Nehemiah 8:10, Then Nehemiah told them, "Go and eat what is rich, drink what is sweet, and send out portions to those who have nothing prepared, since today is holy to our Lord. Do not grieve, for the joy of the Lord is your strength."

moral restoration of his people. The Book of Nehemiah thus underscores themes of restoration and revival, illustrating a leader who, moved by the plight of his people, seeks divine guidance through prayer before embarking on a mission that ultimately revitalizes a community's faith and fortitude. Nehemiah's story shows the power of dedicated leadership and fervent prayer in overcoming despair and renewing a collective commitment to God.

**Personal Notes:**

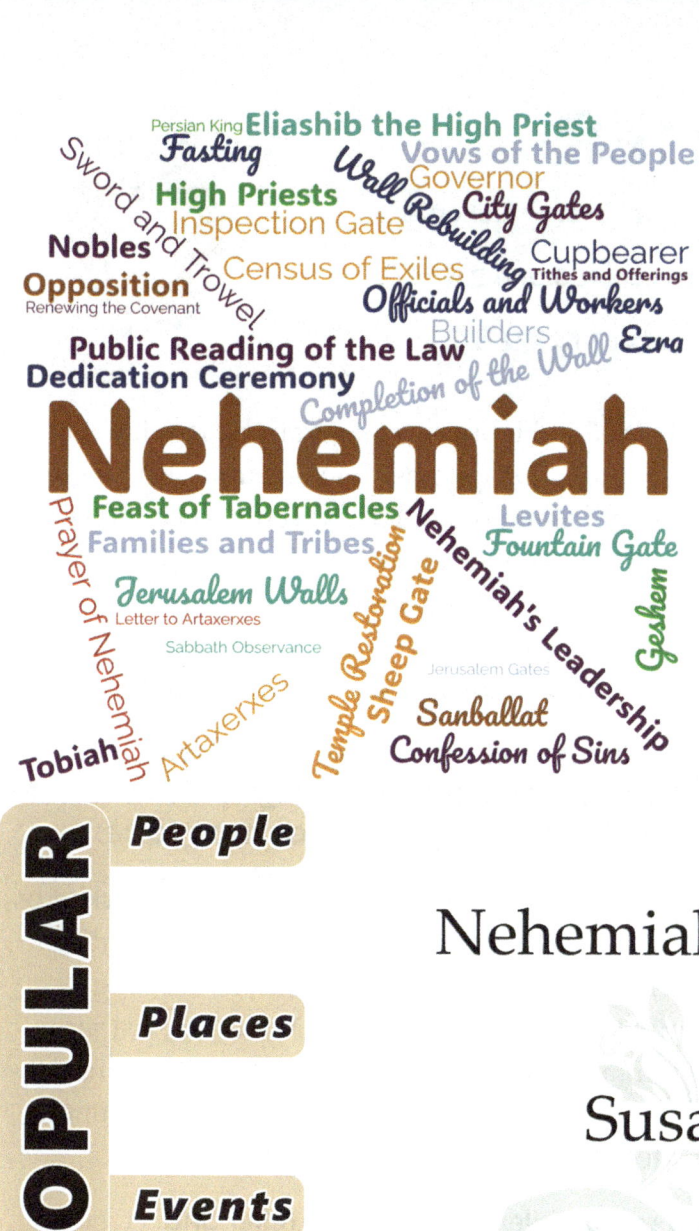

## Reflections on Nehemiah
*Wall Reconstruction*

God's blessings and approval were upon Zerubbabel, Ezra, and Nehemiah as they propelled the post-exilic restoration forward. Amid Israel's faltering revival, Ezra and Nehemiah exemplified unwavering leadership. The Temple and Jerusalem were central in directing God's blessings to His people. For God's people, the route to His blessings was paved with repentance and holiness.

## NOTABLE & POPULAR

**People**

Nehemiah, Ezra, Sanballat

**Places**

Susa, Jerusalem

**Events**

Rebuilding Jerusalem's Walls, Reforms of Nehemiah

**Verses**

**Nehemiah 1:3** And they told me, "The remnant who survived the exile are there in the province, in great trouble and disgrace. The wall of Jerusalem is broken down, and its gates are burned with fire."

**Nehemiah 1:11** O Lord, may Your ear be attentive to my prayer and to the prayers of Your servants who delight to revere Your name. Give Your servant success this day, I pray, and grant him mercy in the sight of this man." (At that time I was the cupbearer to the king.)

**Nehemiah 6:15-16** So the wall was completed in fifty-two days, on the twenty-fifth of Elul. When all our enemies heard about this, all the surrounding nations were afraid and disheartened, for they realized that this task had been accomplished by our God.

# ESTHER

**Author:** Possibly Mordecai, or Ezra, or Nehemiah

**Time Written:** Likely between 460 and 350 B.C.

**Time Covered:** Around 483 to 472 B.C.

Esther, originally named Hadassah which means "Myrtle" in Hebrew, was given the Persian name Ester, derived from the Persian word "stara" meaning "Star." Despite her background as a Hebrew exile, Esther's unique circumstances led her to become the queen of Persia, an ironic twist given her humble origins as an orphan raised by her cousin Mordecai. While Esther's beauty initially captured the king's attention, it was her spiritual integrity that truly endeared her to him, positioning her within the royal court. The Book of Esther is a fascinating narrative filled with intrigue and bravery, and interestingly, it does not explicitly mention God—an aspect that has

**A Key Verse:** Esther 7:3, Queen Esther replied, "If I have found favor in your sight, O king, and if it pleases the king, grant me my life as my petition, and the lives of my people as my request.

sparked debate over its inclusion in the biblical canon. However, the story is profoundly marked by divine providence and protection, particularly evident when the Jewish people face the threat of extermination. Characters like Esther and Mordecai emerge as heroes, while Haman, the king's adviser, plays the villain with his malicious plan against the Jews. Inspired by Mordecai, Esther courageously intervenes, risking her life to thwart Haman's plot. Through Esther's bravery and Mordecai's wisdom, a catastrophic plan is transformed into a triumphant deliverance, a testament to God's unwavering fidelity. The story of Esther underscores that the unseen hand of God

**A Popular Verse:** Esther 4:14, For if you remain silent at this time, relief and deliverance for the Jews will arise from another place, but you and your father's house will perish. And who knows if perhaps you have come to the kingdom for such a time as this?"

orchestrates the deliverance and welfare of His people, employing those who dare to confront adversity in its most daunting forms. This narrative serves as a compelling reminder of how God can turn dire situations into opportunities for blessing, showcasing His profound love and protective power.

**Personal Notes:**

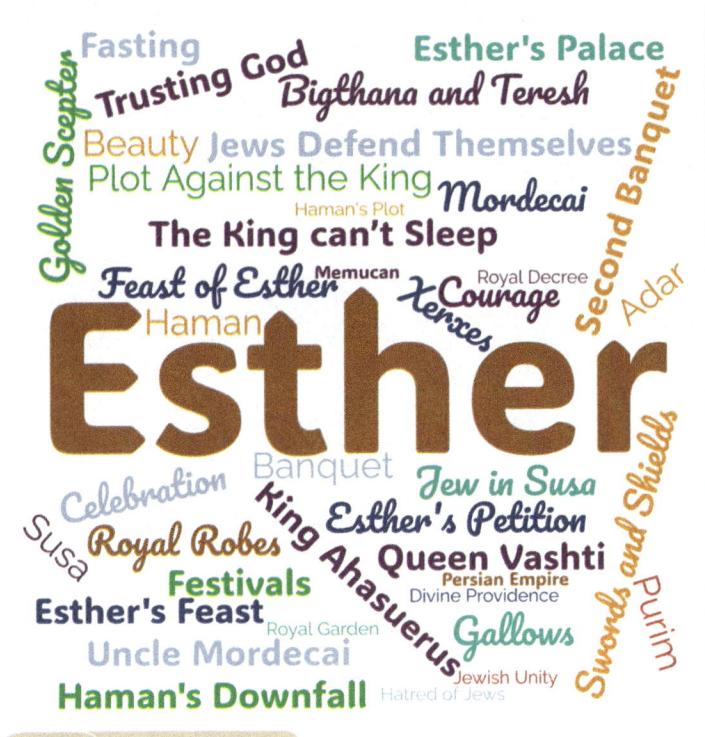

## Reflections on Esther
*Providence and Courage*

God's people may face severe trials under the oppression of their enemies. Yet, God assures them of preservation during these times of hardship. In His mercy, the Lord will reverse the fate of those who torment His people and elevate His own from their lowly situations. Amidst trials and suffering, God's people must rely on Him for support and remain faithful. Furthermore, by recalling and celebrating past instances of God's deliverance, they can draw strength and courage to endure current tribulations.

## NOTABLE & POPULAR

**People**

Esther, Mordecai, Haman, Xerxes

**Places**

Susa

**Events**

Esther Becomes Queen, Jews Saved from Genocide

**Verses**

**Esther 2:15** Now Esther was the daughter of Abihail, the uncle from whom Mordecai had adopted her as his own daughter. And when it was her turn to go to the king, she did not ask for anything except what Hegai, the king's trusted official in charge of the harem, had advised. And Esther found favor in the eyes of everyone who saw her.

**Esther 6:13** Haman told his wife Zeresh and all his friends everything that had happened. His advisers and his wife Zeresh said to him, "Since Mordecai, before whom your downfall has begun, is Jewish, you will not prevail against him—for surely you will fall before him."

**Esther 9:22** as the days on which the Jews gained rest from their enemies and the month in which their sorrow turned to joy and their mourning into a holiday. He wrote that these were to be days of feasting and joy, of sending gifts to one another and to the poor.

# POETRY

## Poetic Books
*Psalms* · *Song of Solomon* · *Job* · *Proverbs* · *Ecclesiastes*

The books of poetry in the Bible, often referred to as God's wisdom literature, offer profound insights and timeless truths. The book of Job is considered the oldest book in the Bible and recounts the story of Job, a man who endured tremendous suffering despite being blameless and upright (Job 1:1,8; 2:3). The other poetic books—Psalms, Proverbs, Ecclesiastes, and the Song of Solomon—were primarily authored by King David and his son Solomon, each bringing unique expressions of worship, wisdom, and reflections on life.

Psalms is a collection of heartfelt prayers and hymns, serving as a rich source of worship. Countless modern songs have drawn inspiration and lyrics from the Psalms, reflecting their enduring impact. Proverbs offers practical wisdom for everyday living, providing guidelines on how to lead a life that honors God. Ecclesiastes explores the existential musings of life on earth, particularly highlighting the emptiness and futility experienced by those who live without faith in God. This book serves as a sobering reflection on the meaning of life from a worldly perspective without divine insight.

The Song of Solomon stands out among these books because it beautifully portrays the courtship and marriage of a man and a woman, celebrating their love and physical relationship. This poetic depiction underscores that God values marriage and affirms the physical aspects of matrimonial love. Through these books, we see God's wisdom at work, offering guidance, comfort, and insight into leading a life that reflects His love and truth. Together, these poetic works draw us closer to understanding God's heart and His intentions for humanity.

**Personal Notes:**

# JOB

**Author:** Likely Job, or Moses, or Solomon

**Time Written:** Sometime between 1440 and 950 B.C.

**Time Covered:** Before 2100 B.C.

Job, potentially the earliest text in the Biblical canon, unfolds during the epoch of biblical patriarchs such as Abraham, Isaac, Jacob, and Joseph. It centers on Job, a man profoundly tested by the loss of his wealth, family, reputation, and health. The narrative opens with a compelling heavenly dialogue between God and Satan, setting the stage for ensuing trials. As the story progresses, it details three intense debates between Job and his companions who seek to understand the cause of his sudden misfortunes. The dialogues delve deep into questions of suffering and divine justice, leading to a climactic point where God Himself intervenes, providing what is often referred to as a "divine

**A Key Verse:** Job 1:21, saying: "Naked I came from my mother's womb, and naked I will return. The Lord gave, and the Lord has taken away. Blessed be the name of the Lord."

diagnosis." Through a series of profound speeches, God does not answer "why" directly but rather challenges Job's understanding of divine omnipotence and wisdom. This pivotal interaction underscores the complexity of God's nature and the limitations of human understanding. In the powerful conclusion of the book, Job acknowledges the sovereignty and supremacy of God in all things, affirming his faith despite his immense hardships. This recognition brings about a restoration, with Job receiving blessings that surpass those he had before his trials. The story of Job, deeply embedded with themes of endurance and faith, reinforces the belief in God's unwavering

**A Popular Verse:** Job 19:25, But I know that my Redeemer lives, and in the end He will stand upon the earth.

sovereignty and His compassionate oversight, even when life presents inexplicable challenges.

**Personal Notes:**

## Reflections on Job
*Suffering and Faith*

Behind every episode of suffering, hidden from our understanding, are God's mysterious purposes. Common sayings may sometimes illuminate situations, but they often fail when confronted with the suffering of the righteous. In such cases, the righteous are urged to blend their laments with affirmations of God's goodness and justice. Human wisdom has its limits, with its humble origins found in our reverence for God and adherence to His commandments.

## NOTABLE & POPULAR

**People**

Job, Eliphaz, Bildad, Zophar

**Places**

Uz

**Events**

Job's Suffering, Debates with Friends, God's Response

**Verses**

**Job 1:1** There was a man in the land of Uz whose name was Job. And this man was blameless and upright, fearing God and shunning evil.

**Job 28:28** And He said to man, 'Behold, the fear of the Lord, that is wisdom, and to turn away from evil is understanding.'"

**Job 38:1-2** Then the Lord answered Job out of the whirlwind and said: "Who is this who obscures My counsel by words without knowledge?

**Job 42:5-6** My ears had heard of You, but now my eyes have seen You. Therefore I retract my words, and I repent in dust and ashes."

**Job 42:10** After Job had prayed for his friends, the Lord restored his prosperity and doubled his former possessions.

# PSALMS

**Author:** Mainly David, with Asaph, Solomon, and Others

**Time Written:** Over many centuries but compiled after 537 B.C

**Time Covered:** around 1407 to 586 B.C.

The Book of Psalms, one of the most cherished and frequently consulted books in the Bible, traverses the complete spectrum of human emotions in a profound and accessible manner. Comprised of 150 sacred songs or "psalms," the range of topics stretches from creation through various historical periods of the Bible. The Psalms address a multitude of subjects such as joy, conflict, peace, worship, divine judgment, expectations concerning the promised Messiah, and personal lamentation. Originally, these psalms were often sung in ancient Israel to the accompaniment of stringed instruments, primarily serving as both hymnal and spiritual meditative

**A Key Verse:** Psalms 121:1-2, I lift up my eyes to the hills. From where does my help come? My help comes from the Lord, the Maker of heaven and earth.

guides in the Temple, particularly after the Jews returned from the Babylonian exile and rebuilt the second temple. Over time, these individual psalms were compiled into what we now recognize as the Book of Psalms. Initially unnamed due to its diverse content, it was eventually termed in Hebrew as Sepher Tehillim, which translates to the "Book of Praises," a fitting title as nearly every psalm includes some form of praise to God. The Greek translation, the Septuagint, refers to it as Psalmoi, highlighting the performative aspect— "Poems Sung to the Accompaniment of Musical Instruments." This term is the root of the term "Psalter," a collection reflected in the English

**A Popular Verse:** Psalms 23:1, The Lord is my shepherd; I shall not want.

language as the Psalter. Among the Old Testament books, Psalms, just behind Isaiah, stands as the most frequently quoted in the New Testament, underscoring its significance in worship, ceremony, and the things of God. Rich in spiritual depth and prophetic insight, many pivotal prophecies concerning Jesus are embedded within the Psalms, including references to what would be His character and mission. Thematically, while the Book of Psalms encompasses a broad array of sacred and existential themes, its core emphasis remains on prayer, praise, and worship—a testament to its enduring role in nurturing the faith and devotion of believers across millennia.

**Personal Notes:**

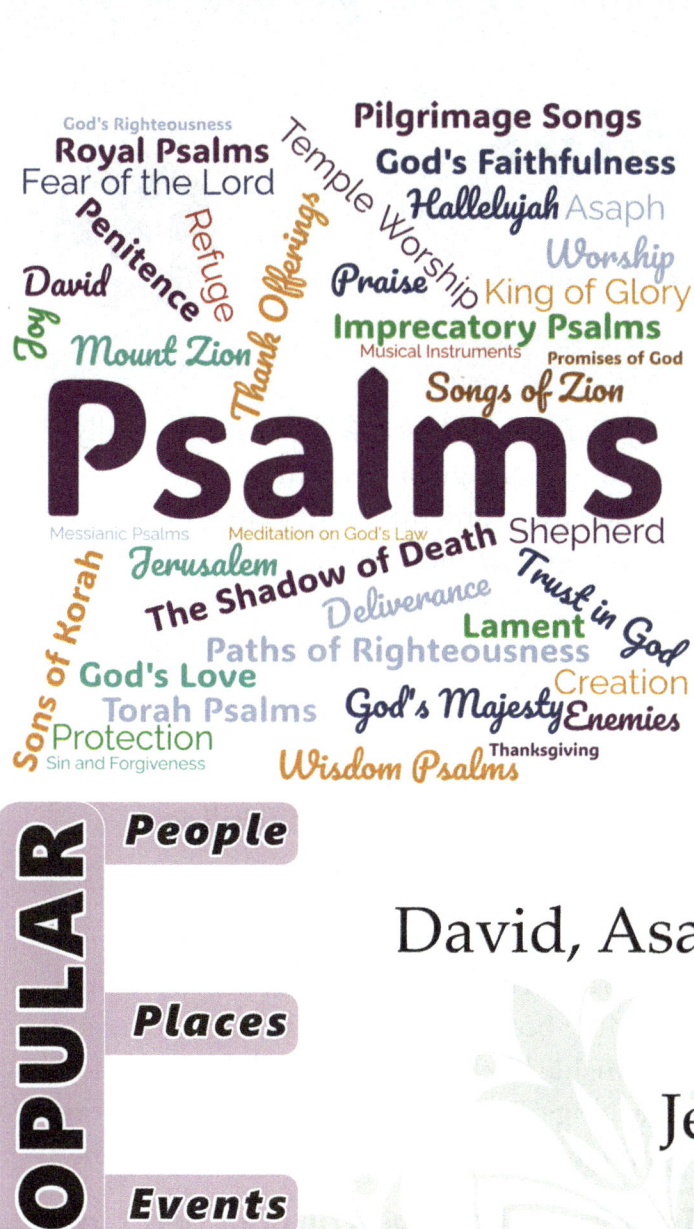

# Reflections on Psalms
*Praise and Worship*

God is deserving of all praise. He is a refuge, safeguarding and rescuing the righteous in times of trouble. His blessings abound in the lives of those who obey Him, whereas judgment is reserved for the disobedient. Worship should be firmly rooted in God's revelations. Genuine worship encompasses a wide range of emotions, stemming from various life experiences.

## NOTABLE & POPULAR

**People**

David, Asaph, Sons of Korah

**Places**

Jerusalem

**Events**

Praises, Laments, Royal Psalms

**Verses**

**Psalm 19:1** The heavens declare the glory of God; the skies proclaim the work of His hands.

**Psalm 22:16-19** For dogs surround me; a band of evil men encircles me; they have pierced my hands and feet. I can count all my bones; they stare and gloat over me. They divide my garments among them and cast lots for my clothing. But You, O Lord, be not far off; O my Strength, come quickly to help me.

**Psalm 51:10** Create in me a clean heart, O God, and renew a right spirit within me.

**Psalm 119:1-2** Blessed are those whose way is blameless, who walk in the Law of the Lord. Blessed are those who keep His testimonies and seek Him with all their heart.

# PROVERBS

**Author:** Mainly Solomon, also Agur and Lemuel

**Time Written:** Around 900 B.C.

**Time Covered:** Around 950 B.C.

The central theme of the Book of Proverbs is "wisdom," defined as the capacity to live life fully in line with God's will and principles. Proverbs addresses the challenge of upholding a godly existence in a secular world, offering spiritual insights on navigating the complexities of daily interactions. The book provides guidance on a variety of personal and social relationships, including those with God, family, neighbors, and authorities, and delves into issues such as pride, laziness, greed, anger, and other moral pitfalls. Solomon, the primary author and a symbol of peak biblical wisdom, crafted these texts to equip the faithful with divine insight necessary for

**A Key Verse:** Proverbs 1:7, The fear of the Lord is the beginning of knowledge, but fools despise wisdom and discipline.

addressing life's varied challenges. Solomon's proverbs convey in essence that living wisely according to God's decrees typically leads to blessings, while folly, characterized by stubbornness and disregard for divine guidance, results in regret and ruin. This relationship between wisdom and outcome is underscored throughout the text, providing both warning and encouragement. Reflecting its authorship, the book's Hebrew name is "Mishle Shelomoh," or "Proverbs of Solomon" (Prov. 1:1), emphasizing its origins from Solomon's teachings. The Latin title "Liber Proverbiorum" structures its name around the concepts of 'for' (Pro) and 'words' (Verba), highlighting how the

**A Popular Verse:** Proverbs 3:5-6, Trust in the Lord with all your heart, and lean not on your own understanding; in all your ways acknowledge Him, and He will make your paths straight.

proverbs distill extensive wisdom into succinct phrases. Proverbs encapsulates the practical application of the Mosaic Law's teachings, rendering them accessible and applicable for everyday life. A recurring phrase within the book, "the fear of the Lord," signifies the foundational theological (or study of 'the things of God') principle that motivates and molds the entire compilation. This reverential attitude towards God is not only the beginning of wisdom but is also portrayed as the way to achieve a successful and righteous life according to the timeless truths of scripture.

**Personal Notes:**

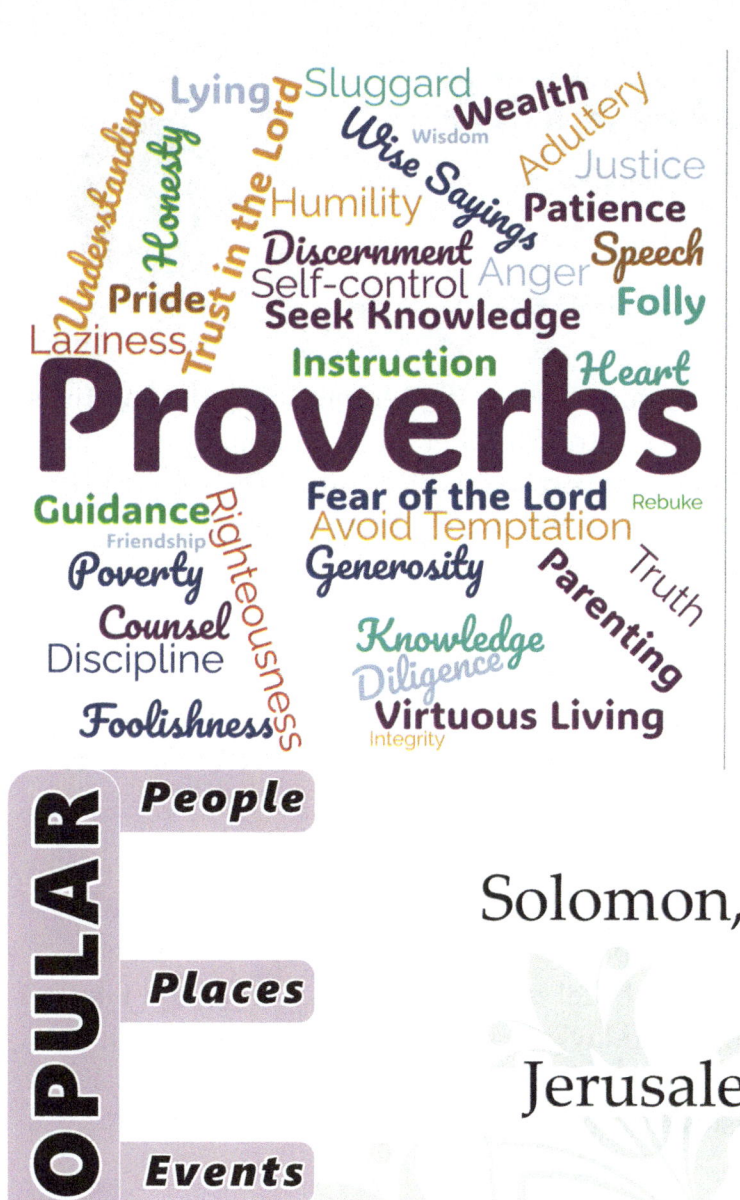

# Reflections on Proverbs
*Wisdom for Living*

God, as the source of all wisdom, affords us the chance to learn and attain it. Acquiring human wisdom is deeply rooted in a reverential respect for God. The mantle of wisdom should be handed down from the elder and more experienced to the younger generation, enriching them with knowledge for their life's journey. Especially, leaders among God's people need thorough instruction in the ways of wisdom.

## NOTABLE & POPULAR

**People**

Solomon, Agur, Lemuel

**Places**

Jerusalem (assumed)

**Events**

Wisdom Sayings

**Verses**

**Proverbs 1:5** let the wise listen and gain instruction, and the discerning acquire wise counsel

**Proverbs 4:5** Get wisdom, get understanding; do not forget my words or turn from them.

**Proverbs 8:13-14** To fear the Lord is to hate evil; I hate arrogant pride, evil conduct, and perverse speech. Counsel and sound judgment are mine; I have insight and strength.

**Proverbs 15:1** A gentle answer turns away wrath, but a harsh word stirs up anger.

**Proverbs 22:6** Train up a child in the way he should go, and when he is old he will not depart from it.

# ECCLESIASTES

**Author:** Likely Solomon

**Time Written:** Around 935 B.C.

**Time Covered:** Around 937 B.C.

The core message of Ecclesiastes revolves around the theme of "vanity," emphasizing the emptiness of seeking happiness without God. Solomon, identified as the Preacher and traditionally recognized as Israel's wisest and richest king, evaluates life from a human standpoint "under the sun" and finds it wholly lacking. He asserts that no amount of power, popularity, prestige, or pleasure can satisfy the deep, God-shaped void in humanity. However, viewed through the lens of divine perspective, life is imbued with significant meaning and purpose, transforming skepticism and despair into joy as we recognize each day as a precious gift from God. The title "Qoheleth", from

**A Key Verse:** Ecclesiastes 12:13, When all has been heard, the conclusion of the matter is this: Fear God and keep His commandments, because this is the whole duty of man.

the Hebrew for "Preacher," derives from 'qahal,' meaning to gather or assemble, fitting for one who speaks before a gathering. The book's Greek title, Ekklesiastes, reflects this as well, meaning one who addresses an assembly or church. Despite its often pessimistic tone, which sparked debate among the ancient Hebrews about its inclusion in the biblical canon, Ecclesiastes remains a vital part of Scripture. Its message resonates particularly in today's secular society, affirming that life devoid of God is ultimately futile—regardless of one's achievements in wealth, fame, or power. Concluding with a timeless exhortation, Ecclesiastes advises us to "Fear God and keep His

**A Popular Verse:** Ecclesiastes 3:1, To everything there is a season, and a time for every purpose under heaven:

commandments, because this is the whole duty of man" (Eccl. 12:13). This profound lesson underscores that outside a vibrant, ongoing relationship with God, even a life marked by worldly "success" is fraught with futility and emptiness. Through its teachings, Ecclesiastes encourages us to seek fulfillment and purpose not in earthly accomplishments, but in our devotion to God and His eternal principles.

**Personal Notes:**

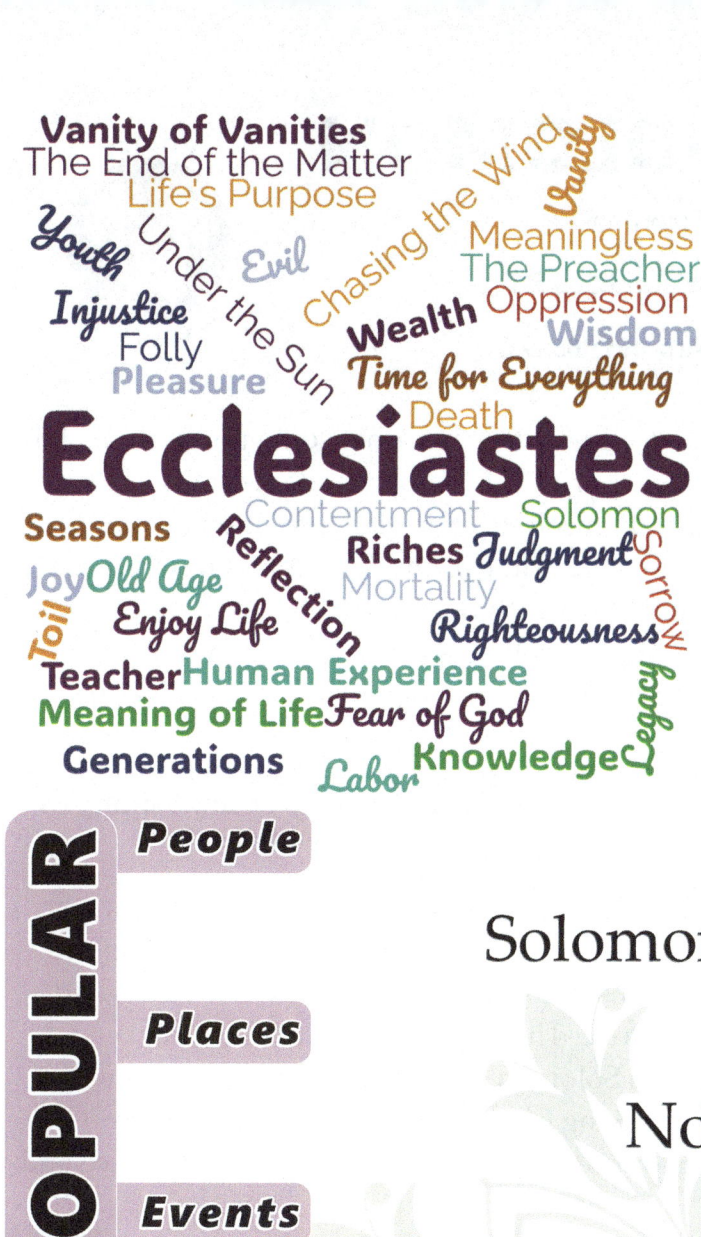

## Reflections on Ecclesiastes
*Life's Meaning*

Left to our own devices, life can appear meaningless and mired in despair, constrained by our limited human perspectives and efforts. The divine wisdom that orchestrates all things remains beyond our full comprehension. Yet, recognizing these limitations allows faith to offer a renewed, godly viewpoint as we reaffirm our reverence for God and commitment to His commands. Ultimately, in His final judgment, God will resolve life's perplexing contradictions by distinguishing good from evil.

## NOTABLE & POPULAR

**People**

Solomon (traditionally)

**Places**

Not specified

**Events**

Reflections on Life's Meaning

**Verses**

**Ecclesiastes 1:2** "Futility of futilities," says the Teacher, "futility of futilities! Everything is futile!"

**Ecclesiastes 1:18** For with much wisdom comes much sorrow, and as knowledge grows, grief increases.

**Ecclesiastes 2:11** Yet when I considered all the works that my hands had accomplished and what I had toiled to achieve, I found everything to be futile, a pursuit of the wind; there was nothing to be gained under the sun.

**Ecclesiastes 12:1** Remember your Creator in the days of your youth, before the days of adversity come and the years approach of which you will say, "I find no pleasure in them,"

# SONG OF SOLOMON

**Author:** Solomon

**Time Written:** Around 965 B.C.

**Time Covered:** Around 965 B.C.

God indeed speaks to us about love, sex, and intimacy, and contrary to what some might think, His message is not merely a series of prohibitions. The Bible portrays love as a fundamental and deeply positive aspect of human experience, designed by God Himself. In fact, scripture often uses the dynamics of human relationships to illustrate divine love. A prime example of this is found in the Song of Solomon, a poetic book that celebrates romantic love with rich metaphors and vivid imagery. The Song of Solomon, written by King Solomon, literally explores the romantic journey between a shepherdess and the king, detailing the excitement, joy, challenges, and depth of married

**A Key Verse:** Song of Solomon 8:6, Set me as a seal over your heart, as a seal upon your arm. For love is as strong as death, its jealousy as unrelenting as Sheol. Its sparks are fiery flames, the fiercest blaze of all.

love. However, beyond its literal interpretation, this book has historically been viewed through an allegorical lens. It has been seen as depicting Israel as God's betrothed bride and symbolizing the church as the bride of Christ. This perspective gives us insight into how deeply God loves us and how our fulfillment can be found in His unconditional love. The book's Hebrew title, "Shir Hashirim," which means "Song of Songs," suggests it is Solomon's finest work, indicating the supreme beauty and importance of love. Therefore, the Song of Solomon not only affirms the sanctity and beauty of human love but also enhances our understanding of God's infinite grace and

**A Popular Verse:** Song of Solomon 2:16, My beloved is mine and I am his; he pastures his flock among the lilies.

mercy. By celebrating the joys that husbands and wives experience through romantic love, it mirrors the divine love God extends to us, His people. Thus, our loving relationships here on earth can reflect and point us to the deeper, eternal love relationship with God through Christ. This divine connection, as illustrated in the Bible, underscores that God's teachings on love are not restrictive but are invitations to experience love in its fullest and most beautiful form.

**Personal Notes:**

## Reflections on Song of Solomon
*Love and Marriage*

God's marvelous gift to humanity is the romantic love that blossoms between a husband and wife. Within the sanctity of marriage, men and women are intended to discover both emotional and physical joy and fulfillment in one another's presence.

## NOTABLE & POPULAR

**People**

Solomon, the Shulammite

**Places**

Jerusalem (assumed)

**Events**

Love and Marriage Poems

**Verses**

**Song of Solomon 1:2** Let him kiss me with the kisses of his mouth! For your love is more delightful than wine.

**Song of Solomon 5:1** I have come to my garden, my sister, my bride; I have gathered my myrrh with my spice. I have eaten my honeycomb with my honey; I have drunk my wine with my milk. Eat, O friends, and drink; drink freely, O beloved.

**Song of Solomon 8:4** O daughters of Jerusalem, I adjure you: Do not arouse or awaken love until the time is right.

**Song of Solomon 8:7** Mighty waters cannot quench love; rivers cannot sweep it away. If a man were to give all the wealth of his house for love, his offer would be utterly scorned.

# MAJOR PROPHETS

## Lamentations
## Major Prophets
### Isaiah
### Daniel
### Jeremiah
### Ezekiel

The major prophets—Isaiah, Jeremiah, Lamentations, Ezekiel, and Daniel—are considered "major" not due to their prophetic significance but because of their extended length compared to the shorter "minor" prophets. It's essential to remember that all prophetic books were inspired by the Holy Spirit, making each one equally important in the eyes of God.

The book of Isaiah, written between 700 and 671 B.C., predates the Babylonian conquest of Judah. Isaiah's message was a call for repentance, warning both the northern and southern kingdoms of impending judgment due to their sins. Despite these warnings, the northern kingdom fell to the Assyrian army. Isaiah also contains profound prophecies about Israel's return to their land, the first and second comings of Christ, the future millennial kingdom, and the eternal state. Jeremiah's writings, spanning 586 to 570 B.C., reflect the period of Babylonian captivity. The book of Lamentations, dated around 586 B.C., mourns the fall of Jerusalem. Similarly, Ezekiel, written between 590 and 570 B.C., addresses the exiles in Babylon, offering hope and calling for faithfulness.

All five major prophets proclaimed God's messages primarily to the southern kingdom of Judah for being unfaithful and not listening to Him. God also expressed His unwavering love and faithfulness, despite the people's rebellion. His warnings were not just about punishment but also carried promises of restoration and future hope for Israel. These books underscore God's ongoing relationship with His chosen people and His ultimate plan of redemption through Jesus Christ. The prophecies stretch far beyond immediate historical events, pointing to Christ's first coming, His future second coming, millennial reign, and the eternal state, reassuring believers of God's sovereign control and redemptive purposes throughout history.

**Personal Notes:**

# ISAIAH

**Author:** Isaiah

**Time Written:** Between 739 and 681 B.C

**Time Covered:** Around 739 to 701 B.C.

The structure of the book of Isaiah mirrors the Bible as a whole, divided into two distinct sections that respectively echo the themes of the Old and New Testaments. The first thirty-nine chapters, like the thirty-nine books of the Old Testament, primarily focus on judgment. These chapters describe the sins of Judah, the surrounding nations, and the entire earth, portraying a world steeped in moral decay and idolatry. Isaiah's message is clear: God's judgment is inevitable because He cannot tolerate such blatant disobedience indefinitely. Conversely, the final twenty-seven chapters of Isaiah echo the twenty-seven books of the New Testament, shifting to a message of hope and restoration.

**A Key Verse:** Isaiah 53:5, But He was pierced for our transgressions, He was crushed for our iniquities; the punishment that brought us peace was upon Him, and by His stripes we are healed.

These chapters foretell the coming of the Messiah, who will serve both as a suffering Savior and a reigning Sovereign. This future king will not only rescue God's people but also transform their hearts, enabling them to follow Him wholeheartedly. The restoration and blessings promised herein highlight God's steadfast purpose to redeem and renew His creation. Isaiah's name, meaning "Yahweh is salvation," encapsulates the book's overarching theme: salvation comes from God alone, not based on human merit but on His own name and magnificent love. Isaiah, recognized as perhaps the greatest of the Old Testament prophets due to his clear messianic prophecies and his

**A Popular Verse:** Isaiah 40:31, But those who wait upon the Lord will renew their strength; they will mount up with wings like eagles; they will run and not grow weary, they will walk and not faint.

extensive ministry during the reign of four kings, conveys a profound message. Even in judgment, God's commitment to preserve a faithful remnant underscores His redemptive plan for humanity— a theme vividly portrayed in Isaiah's visions of an age when the earth will be filled with the knowledge of the Lord. This dual message of righteous judgment and hopeful salvation runs throughout the book, presenting a comprehensive view of God's character and plans.

**Personal Notes:**

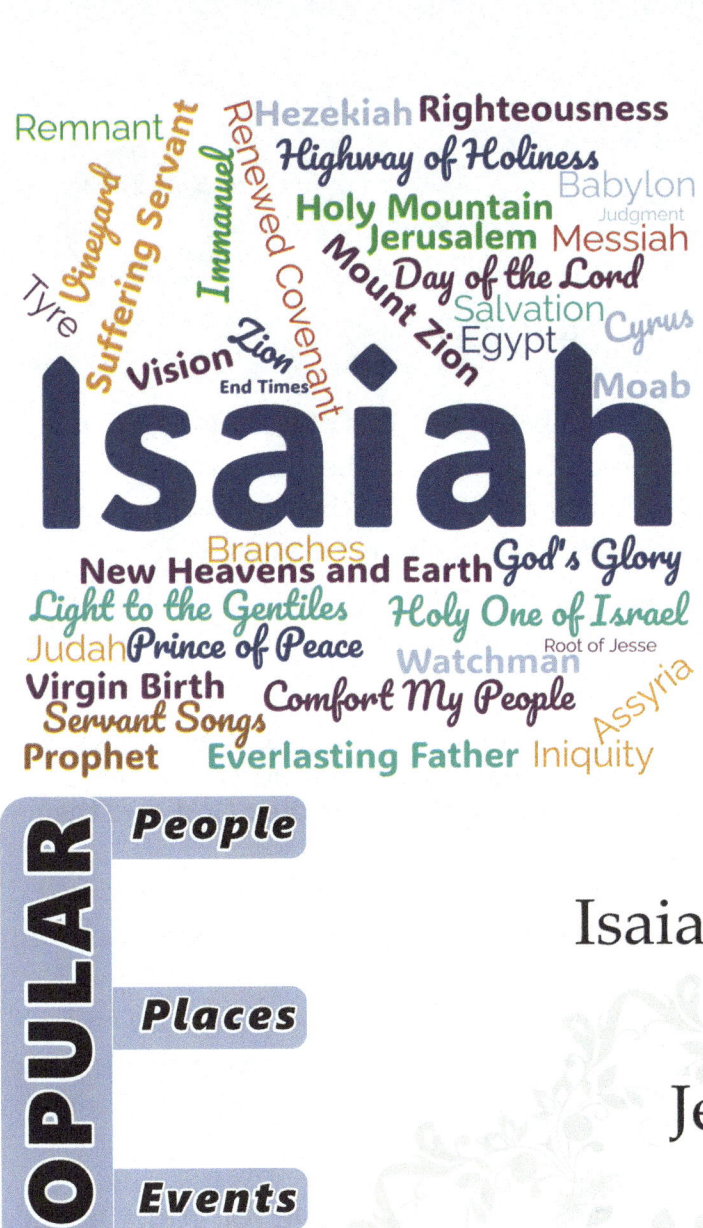

## Reflections on Isaiah
*Salvation and Judgment*

Isaiah was divinely appointed to warn His people of the coming exile while also offering them hope of a prosperous restoration afterward. The fulfillment of Isaiah's earlier prophecies, evident by the time of the book's writing, solidified his credibility. His extraordinary predictions about the end of the Babylonian exile and the ensuing restoration were certain to come to pass, yet only the repentant in Israel and other nations would experience these future blessings.

## Notable & Popular

**People**

Isaiah, Hezekiah

**Places**

Jerusalem

**Events**

Prophecies of Judgment and Redemption

**Verses**

**Isaiah 6:8** Then I heard the voice of the Lord saying: "Whom shall I send? Who will go for Us?" And I said: "Here am I. Send me!"

**Isaiah 7:14** Therefore the Lord Himself will give you a sign: Behold, the virgin will be with child and will give birth to a son, and will call Him Immanuel.

**Isaiah 9:6** For unto us a child is born, unto us a son is given, and the government will be upon His shoulders. And He will be called Wonderful Counselor, Mighty God, Everlasting Father, Prince of Peace.

**Isaiah 65:25** The wolf and the lamb will feed together, and the lion will eat straw like the ox, but the food of the serpent will be dust. They will neither harm nor destroy on all My holy mountain," says the Lord.

# JEREMIAH

**Author:** Jeremiah

**Time Written:** Between 630 and 580 B.C.

**Time Covered:** Around 627 to 586 B.C.

The Book of Jeremiah chronicles the profound and often somber prophecies of Jeremiah, a young man from the priestly town of Anathoth, who was called by God into a challenging prophetic ministry. The name Jeremiah, or Yirmeyahu in Hebrew, meaning "Yahweh throws," suggests a sense of "Yahweh establishing or appointing." Reflecting this, Jeremiah's mission was one of establishing God's messages of impending judgment to the people of Judah, a task he undertook for over forty years. Known poignantly as "the weeping prophet," Jeremiah's ministry was marked by his deep sorrow and compassion. Despite his relentless warnings of doom, the people of Judah,

**A Key Verse:** Jeremiah 31:33, "But this is the covenant I will make with the house of Israel after those days, declares the Lord. I will put My law in their minds and inscribe it on their hearts. And I will be their God, and they will be My people.

including their kings, consistently rejected his counsel. This rejection only extended his prophetic mission as he continued to call for repentance, making his book even lengthier after King Jehoiakim burned the initial scroll containing Jeremiah's prophecies, prompting him to rewrite and expand them. His tears of compassion imbued his stern messages with a poignant sense of urgency and sorrow. Jeremiah's prophecies focused on the rampant desertion of God by His chosen people, their impending bondage under the Babylonians, and ultimately their restoration through God's mercy and grace. He criticized both religious and civil leaders for deviating from God's commands,

**A Popular Verse:** Jeremiah 29:11, For I know the plans I have for you, declares the Lord, plans to prosper you and not to harm you, to give you a future and a hope.

replacing divine directives with their own corrupt practices. Through vivid sermons and memorable visual lessons, Jeremiah tirelessly proclaimed that submission to God's will was the only path to avert disaster and secure divine blessing. His ministry, though fraught with personal suffering and rejection, paints a compelling picture of God's relentless pursuit of His people, aiming to turn their hearts back to Him through judgment and grace.

**Personal Notes:**

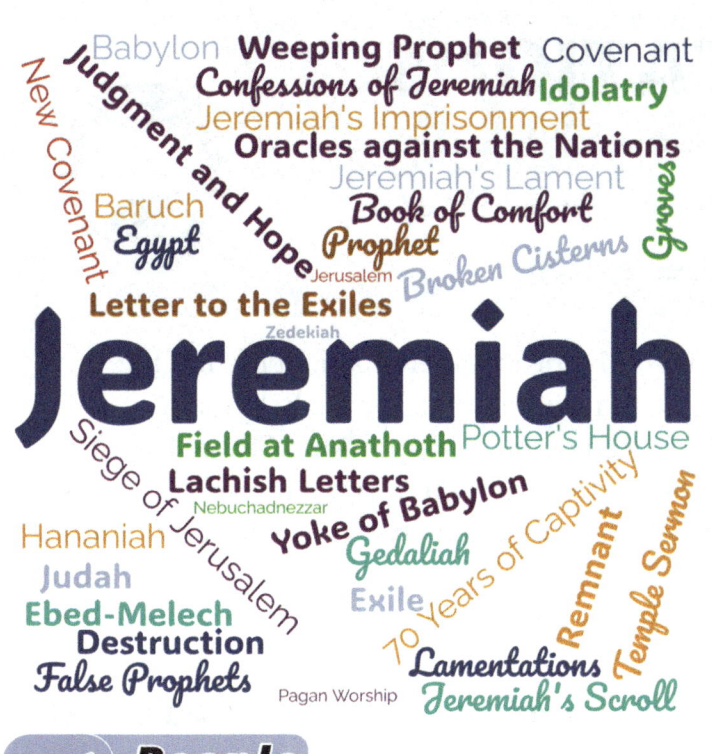

# Reflections on Jeremiah
*Prophecy and Lament*

The exile of Judah and Jerusalem to Babylon was a just consequence of their ongoing sin. Not even the Temple in Jerusalem could protect the Judahites from God's retributive judgment against their hypocrisy. False prophets offering false assurances of peace and safety needed to be rejected in favor of the messages from true prophets. Following the judgment of exile, a magnificent restoration under the auspices of a New Covenant would unfold.

## NOTABLE & POPULAR

**People**

Jeremiah, Baruch

**Places**

Jerusalem, Babylon

**Events**

Prophecies of Judah's Exile, New Covenant Promised

**Verses**

**Jeremiah 1:5** "Before I formed you in the womb I knew you, and before you were born I set you apart and appointed you as a prophet to the nations."

**Jeremiah 17:9** The heart is deceitful above all things and beyond cure. Who can understand it?

**Jeremiah 29:10** For this is what the Lord says: "When Babylon's seventy years are complete, I will attend to you and confirm My promise to restore you to this place.

**Jeremiah 52:12-13** On the tenth day of the fifth month, in the nineteenth year of Nebuchadnezzar's reign over Babylon, Nebuzaradan captain of the guard, a servant of the king of Babylon, entered Jerusalem. He burned down the house of the Lord, the royal palace, and all the houses of Jerusalem—every significant building.

# LAMENTATIONS

**Author:** Jeremiah

**Time Written:** Likely between 586 and 575 B.C.

**Time Covered:** 586 B.C.

*Lamentations — Old Testament*

*Major Prophets — Books 23 - 27*

Lamentations poignantly captures the profound grief of the prophet Jeremiah, depicting the catastrophic fall of Jerusalem and the subsequent exile of its inhabitants by the Babylonians. This book serves as a solemn reflection on the devastation faced by the once-glorious City of David, now reduced to ruins. Jeremiah's heart-wrenching response to the destruction and suffering around him is articulated through five mournful poems, laying bare the raw intensity of his emotions amid the desolation. Throughout Lamentations, Jeremiah's profound sorrow is intermingled with moments of hope as he proclaims, "great is Your faithfulness!" (Lam. 3:23). In the shadow of immense loss

**A Key Verse:** Lamentations 3:40, Let us examine and test our ways, and turn back to the Lord.

and despair, the prophet turns to the enduring mercy, compassion, and goodness of God. Even as he mourns, his faith in God's unceasing fidelity provides a beacon of light. Jeremiah's steadfast belief that the Lord had never failed him, nor ever would, underscores a powerful message of divine reliability and steadfastness in times of deep distress. The book's Hebrew title, "Ekah" (an exclamative "how!"), reflects the lamenting tone, and "qinot" ("Elegies" or "Lamentations") conveys the nature of its content. Echoed in Jerome's Latin Vulgate (an early and important 5th century version of the Holy Bible, in Latin) as "Id est lamentationes Jeremiae prophetae," these titles

**A Popular Verse:** Lamentations 3:22-23, Because of the loving devotion of the Lord we are not consumed, for His mercies never fail. They are new every morning; great is Your faithfulness!

frame the text as a profound expression of mourning and loss. The overriding theme of Lamentations reminds us that adversity often follows unrepented sin. Yet, even in the darkest moments, Jeremiah's focus shifts from the tragedy at hand to the unwavering faithfulness of God, providing a model of hope and comfort that affirms God's commitment to those who love and obey Him, despite the surrounding chaos.

**Personal Notes:**

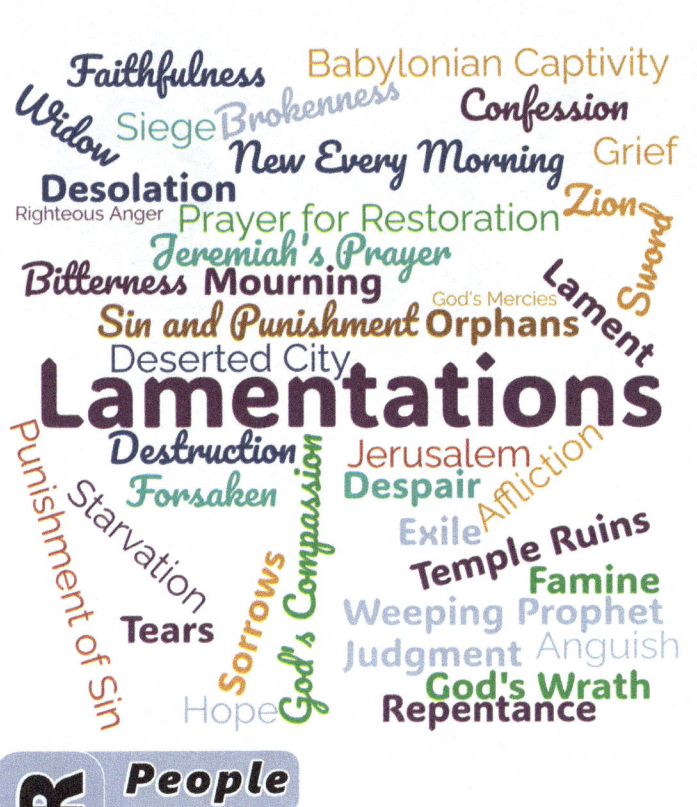

## Reflections on Lamentations
*Mourning and Hope*

Judah and Jerusalem merited the divine judgment they received. The suffering from their destruction and exile was overwhelming, impossible to endure without cries of lamentation. In the midst of such anguish, their only glimmer of hope for deliverance was to appeal to God's mercy.

## NOTABLE & POPULAR

**People**

Jeremiah (traditionally)

**Places**

Jerusalem

**Events**

Laments over Jerusalem's Destruction

**Verses**

**Lamentations 2:17** The Lord has done what He planned; He has accomplished His decree, which He ordained in days of old; He has overthrown you without pity. He has let the enemy gloat over you and exalted the horn of your foes.

**Lamentations 3:22** Because of the loving devotion of the Lord we are not consumed, for His mercies never fail.

**Lamentations 3:24** "The Lord is my portion," says my soul, "therefore I will hope in Him."

**Lamentations 5:19-22** You, O Lord, reign forever; Your throne endures from generation to generation. Why have You forgotten us forever? Why have You forsaken us for so long? Restore us to Yourself, O Lord, so we may return; renew our days as of old, unless You have utterly rejected us and remain angry with us beyond measure.

# EZEKIEL

**Author:** Ezekiel

**Time Written:** Likely between 593 and 565 B.C.

**Time Covered:** Around 593 to 573 B.C.

Ezekiel, both a priest and prophet, served during Judah's harrowing seventy years of Babylonian captivity, marking some of the darkest days in the nation's history. Transported to Babylon prior to Jerusalem's ultimate destruction, Ezekiel communicated God's word to the exiled Jews through prophecies, parables, and vivid object lessons. One of the most poignant images he used was that of dry bones in the sun, symbolizing the desolation of God's people but also prophesying their eventual rejuvenation and restoration as God promises to breathe life into them once more (Ezek. 37:1-14). The name Ezekiel, or Yehezke'l in Hebrew, means "God strengthens," a fitting testament to

**A Key Verse:** Ezekiel 2:3, "Son of man," He said to me, "I am sending you to the Israelites, to a rebellious nation that has rebelled against Me. To this very day they and their fathers have rebelled against Me.

the divine empowerment he received for his daunting role (Ezek. 3:8, 9). His prophetic messages often complement those of Jeremiah; while Jeremiah focused primarily on Judah's impending judgment and ruin, Ezekiel's prophecy heralds renewal and hope. He assures the exiles that their current suffering and judgment would eventually make way for a future filled with glory, intended to affirm God's sovereignty and their understanding when God says: "I am the LORD" (Ezek. 6:7). A significant portion of Ezekiel's writings (chapters 40-48) is dedicated to the detailed description of a future temple with architectural features unlike any previous temples, suggesting its divine

**A Popular Verse:** Ezekiel 36:26, I will give you a new heart and put a new spirit within you; I will remove your heart of stone and give you a heart of flesh.

importance in God's overall plan. In Ezekiel's vision, this temple becomes the everlasting dwelling place of God among His people, asserting, "This is the place of My throne and the place for the soles of My feet, where I will dwell among the Israelites forever" (Ezek. 43:7). Moreover, the city itself is to be renamed "THE LORD IS THERE" (48:35), signifying God's permanent presence and covenant with His people. Through Ezekiel's visions and messages, the theme resoundingly echoes God's promise to restore His people when they turn back to Him and commit their hearts fully to His ways.

**Personal Notes:**

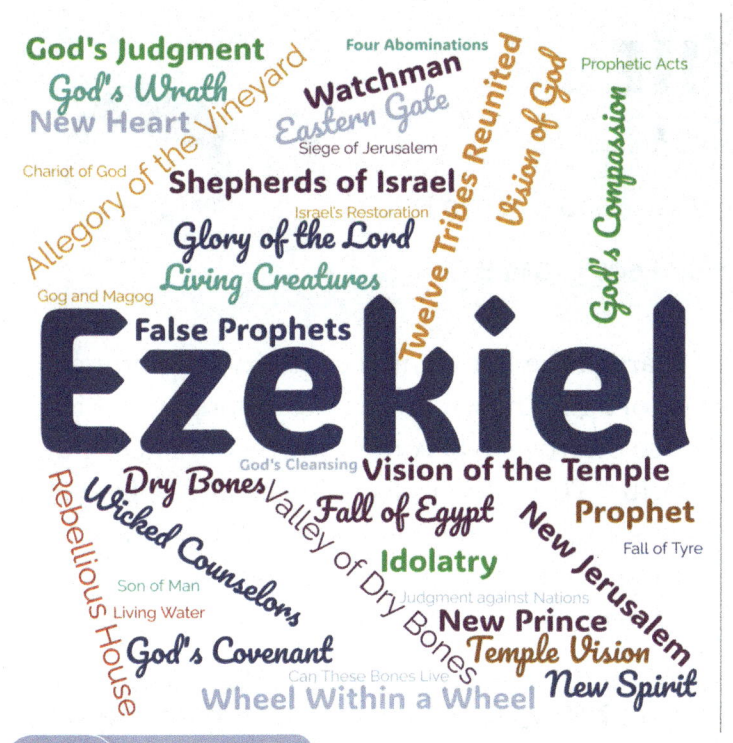

# Reflections on Ezekiel
*Visions and Restoration*

Judah and Jerusalem were rightly subjected to the devastating judgment of utter destruction and exile because of their blatant defiance of God's laws. God promised to bring justice to the nations that tormented His people. After the exile, His people were assured abundant blessings. Jerusalem and its Temple, the core of God's renewed people, would once again thrive with life and devotion.

## NOTABLE & POPULAR

**People**

Ezekiel

**Places**

Babylon, Temple

**Events**

Visions of God's Glory, Dry Bones

**Verses**

**Ezekiel 28:12-14** "Son of man, take up a lament for the king of Tyre and tell him that this is what the Lord GOD says: 'You were the seal of perfection, full of wisdom and perfect in beauty. You were in Eden, the garden of God. Every kind of precious stone adorned you: ruby, topaz, and diamond, beryl, onyx, and jasper, sapphire, turquoise, and emerald. Your mountings and settings were crafted in gold, prepared on the day of your creation. You were anointed as a guardian cherub, for I had ordained you. You were on the holy mountain of God; you walked among the fiery stones.

**Ezekiel 33:11** Say to them: 'As surely as I live, declares the Lord GOD, I take no pleasure in the death of the wicked, but rather that the wicked should turn from their ways and live. Turn! Turn from your evil ways! For why should you die, O house of Israel?'

67

# DANIEL

**Author:** Daniel

**Time Written:** Likely between 540 and 530 B.C.

**Time Covered:** Around 605 to 539 B.C.

Daniel's remarkable life spanned the entire seventy years of the Babylonian captivity, beginning with his deportation to Babylon at about sixteen years of age. Chosen for his exceptional qualities, Daniel was not only integrated into government service but rose to become a prime minister under multiple rulers: Nebuchadnezzar, Belshazzar, and Darius. Throughout his political career, Daniel remained a steadfast prophetic voice, articulating God's sovereign will to both Gentile and Jewish audiences. His influence was so profound that even these monarchs recognized and proclaimed the supremacy of Daniel's God as the singular, living God over all. The name Daniel, deriving from the

**A Key Verse:** Daniel 2:20-21, and declared: "Blessed be the name of God forever and ever, for wisdom and power belong to Him. He changes the times and seasons; He removes kings and establishes them. He gives wisdom to the wise and knowledge to the discerning.

Hebrew "Daniye'l," meaning "God is my Judge," underpins the central theme of the Book of Daniel: divine sovereignty and judgment. This theme is mirrored in the narratives and visions recounted throughout the text, which includes significant prophecies—some of which Jesus Himself referenced (Matthew 24:15). Daniel's experiences, like surviving the lion's den and his friends' miraculous preservation in the fiery furnace, transcend mere children's tales. They are potent, adult-level reminders of God's immediate response to the faithfulness of His followers. Moreover, Daniel's visions extend to prophecies concerning the rise of the Antichrist and the triumphant

**A Popular Verse:** Daniel 3:17-18, If the God whom we serve exists, then He is able to deliver us from the blazing fiery furnace and from your hand, O king. But even if He does not, let it be known to you, O king, that we will not serve your gods or worship the golden statue you have set up."

Second Coming of Christ, linking the Book of Daniel closely with the New Testament's Book of Revelation due to their shared vivid, apocalyptic imagery. Both books emphasize that God's authority supersedes all earthly powers. Through Daniel's life and the book itself, the overarching message is clear: God governs the fate of nations and individuals alike, and His divine purposes are unthwartable. This reassurance of God's absolute sovereignty over human affairs provides a foundational perspective for believers navigating the complexities of faith in every era.

**Personal Notes:**

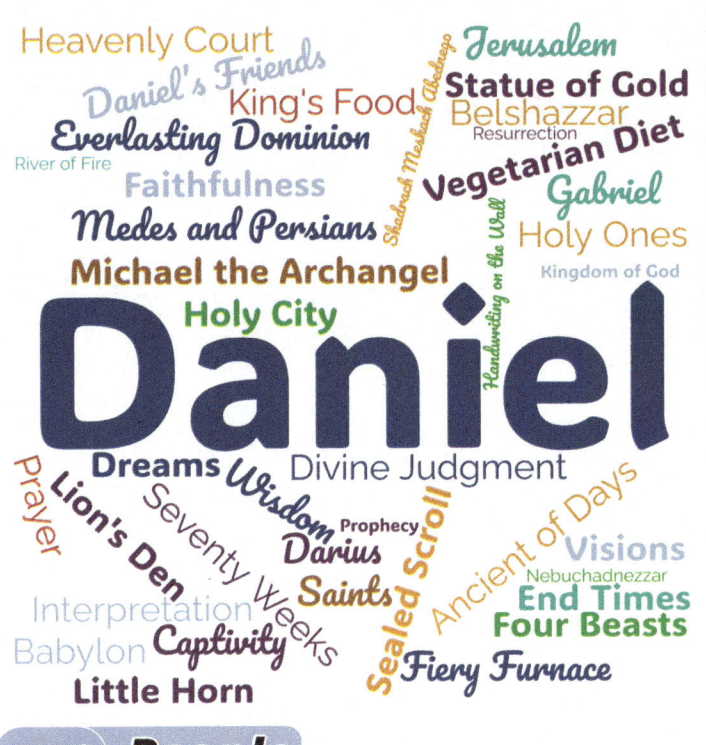

# Reflections on Daniel
*Faithfulness in Exile*

During their exile, Daniel and his friends exhibited steadfast loyalty to God. Daniel's unwavering resolve in the face of his captors bolstered the credibility of his truth-telling. The all-powerful God maintains sovereign control over all of history. Israel's prolonged exile, a consequence of persistent sin, extended through the rule of four kingdoms over God's people. Despite the looming trials, the promise of the Anointed One, the Christ, bringing salvation continued to shine as a beacon of hope.

## NOTABLE & POPULAR

**People**

Daniel, Nebuchadnezzar, Belshazzar

**Places**

Babylon

**Events**

Fiery Furnace, Lion's Den, Prophetic Visions

**Verses**

**Daniel 1:19-20** And the king spoke with them, and among all the young men he found no one equal to Daniel, Hananiah, Mishael, and Azariah. So they entered the king's service. In every matter of wisdom and understanding about which the king consulted them, he found them ten times better than all the magicians and enchanters in his entire kingdom.

**Daniel 4:34-35** But at the end of those days I, Nebuchadnezzar, looked up to heaven, and my sanity was restored to me. Then I praised the Most High, and I honored and glorified Him who lives forever: "For His dominion is an everlasting dominion, and His kingdom endures from generation to generation. All the peoples of the earth are counted as nothing, and He does as He pleases with the army of heaven and the peoples of the earth. There is no one who can restrain His hand or say to Him, 'What have You done?'"

# MINOR PROPHETS

Habakkuk  Jonah  Haggai  Obediah  Malachi  Micah
## Minor Prophets
Amos  Zephaniah  Hosea  Zechariah  Joel
Nahum

The books of the minor prophets, written between 840 and 430 B.C., are as diverse in their messages as they are united in their divine origin. Although details about the lives of some of these prophets remain unknown, their messages are clear. They delivered warnings to Israel and other nations, foretold the coming of the Messiah, and spoke about the future of Israel. These smaller, yet profound, books contribute richly to the tapestry of Old Testament prophecy.

The Old Testament concludes with the book of Malachi, which contains a significant promise: a messenger will precede the arrival of the Messiah—Jesus the Christ. In the final verses, Malachi foretells that Elijah the prophet will come before the great and terrible day of the Lord. This prophecy created an air of anticipation and hope, which lingered during the 400 years of silence that followed. This intertestamental period (the period between the Old and New Testament books) heightened the sense of expectancy for the promised deliverer, setting the stage for the New Testament.

The New Testament picks up where the Old Testament leaves off, continuing the history of the promised One—Jesus the Christ. It begins with the fulfillment of the long-awaited prophecies, starting with John the Baptist's role as the forerunner, resonating with the spirit of Elijah, and leading to the arrival of Jesus. The life, ministry, death, and resurrection of Jesus fulfill the Old Testament prophecies and bring God's redemptive plan to fruition, bridging the gap between the Testaments and affirming the unified story of God's salvation plan for humanity.

**Personal Notes:**

# HOSEA

**Author:** Hosea

**Time Written:** Likely between 755 and 725 B.C.

**Time Covered:** Around 753 B.C.

Hosea's prophetic ministry to the northern kingdom of Israel came during an outwardly prosperous era, yet beneath the surface, the nation was rotting with moral decay and spiritual infidelity. God's directive to Hosea to marry Gomer, a woman known for her promiscuity, set the stage for a powerful, living parable of the unfaithfulness of God's people. This poignant personal life experience helped Hosea deliver his messages with profound empathy and urgency. The naming of his children Lo-Ruhamah ("no mercy") and Lo-Ammi ("not my people") served as stark, symbolic messages to Israel, illustrating the severe consequences of their spiritual estrangement from God.

**A Key Verse:** Hosea 1:2, When the Lord first spoke through Hosea, He told him, "Go, take a prostitute as your wife and have children of adultery, because this land is flagrantly prostituting itself by departing from the Lord."

Throughout his long service, spanning about fifty years, Hosea consistently communicated a threefold message: God's deep abhorrence of sin, the inevitability of divine judgment, and the unchanging nature of His loyal love. Even as Hosea prophesied the harsh reality of punishment—fulfilled through the catastrophic Assyrian invasion in 722 B.C.—he also assured the people of God's unwavering commitment to them. His prophetic promise anticipated a time of restoration and reconciliation, where God would once again gather His people, renew their hearts, and bless them abundantly. The name Hosea, sharing historically in word origin with the names of Joshua

**A Popular Verse:** Hosea 6:6, For I desire mercy, not sacrifice, and the knowledge of God rather than burnt offerings.

and Jesus, stems from the Hebrew root word for "salvation," with the latter names enhancing this to mean "Yahweh is salvation." Hosea's call to the Israelites was clear: if they turned from their idols and returned to God, they would find deliverance. The Book of Hosea, with its intense portrayal of divine love amidst human betrayal, serves as a compelling testament to God's unrelenting effort to reclaim His wayward people. This narrative underscores a vital thematic truth: despite the severe repercussions of spiritual adultery, God's foundational love and commitment to His covenant people remain unshakable.

**Personal Notes:**

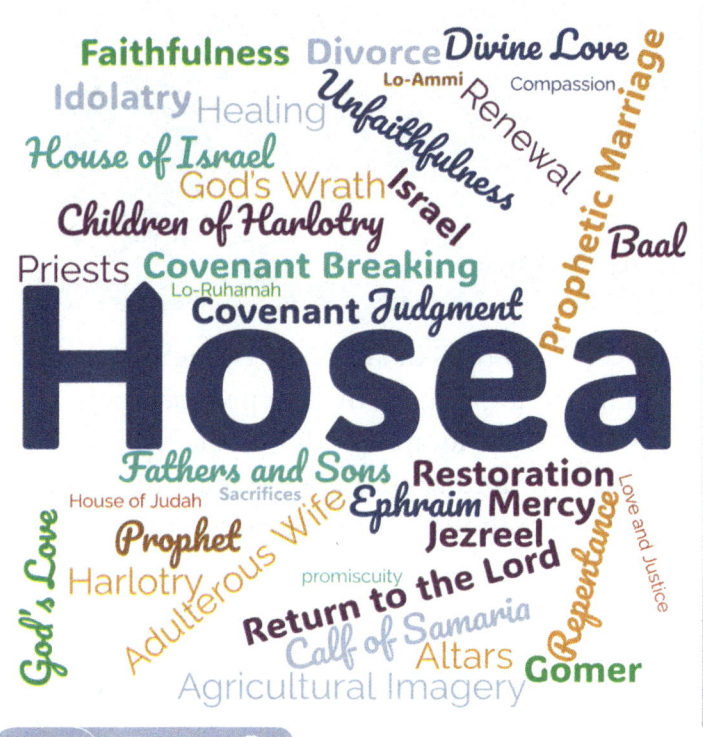

## Reflections on Hosea
*Unfaithfulness and Love*

God embodies the role of a devoted husband, with His people as His cherished bride. Despite His generous benevolence, His people frequently turn away from Him. For their brazen violations of His covenant, God will administer punishment. Nevertheless, His love is steadfast and boundless; He will never fully forsake them. Instead, He promises to restore them to a life of covenant blessings with Him.

## NOTABLE & POPULAR

**People**

Hosea

**Places**

Israel

**Events**

Marriage to Gomer, Prophecies Against Israel

**Verses**

**Hosea 2:23** And I will sow her as My own in the land, and I will have compassion on 'No Compassion.' I will say to those called 'Not My People,' 'You are My people,' and they will say, 'You are my God.'"

**Hosea 14:2-4** Bring your confessions and return to the Lord. Say to Him: "Take away all our iniquity and receive us graciously, that we may present the fruit of our lips. Assyria will not save us, nor will we ride on horses. We will never again say, 'Our gods!' to the work of our own hands. For in You the fatherless find compassion." I will heal their apostasy; I will freely love them, for My anger has turned away from them.

# JOEL

**Author:** Joel

**Time Written:** Likely between 835 and 800 B.C.

**Time Covered:** Around 835 B.C.

*Old Testament*

*Minor Prophets — Books 28 - 39*

The biblical book of Joel powerfully illustrates the dire consequences of sin through the imagery of a locust plague devastating Judah, symbolizing God's impending judgment. The prophet Joel, whose name itself declares that "Yahweh is God," emphasizes the looming "day of the LORD" as a time of severe trial where few can stand. Joel's message is clear and urgent: the people must return to God with heartfelt repentance to avoid the severity of His judgment. He encourages them to turn inward and sincerely rend their hearts, not just outwardly express sorrow, revealing God's desire for genuine transformation (Joel 2:11-14). In this call to repentance, Joel imparts hope alongside the

**A Key Verse:** Joel 2:13, So rend your hearts and not your garments, and return to the Lord your God. For He is gracious and compassionate, slow to anger, abounding in loving devotion. And He relents from sending disaster.

warning. If the people of Judah turn back to God and forsake their sinful ways, they might experience His mercy and receive a blessing in place of deserved destruction. Joel stresses that God is gracious and compassionate, willing to relent from sending calamity if His people show true repentance. This duality of God's character—as both just judge and merciful savior—is central to Joel's message and resonates deeply with all who seek to align their lives with God's will. Joel's relevance extends beyond his historical context, echoing into the New Testament, where Peter cites Joel's prophecy on the Day of Pentecost (Acts 2:16-21). Here, the fulfillment of God's promise

**A Popular Verse:** Joel 2:28, And afterward, I will pour out My Spirit on all people. Your sons and daughters will prophesy, your old men will dream dreams, your young men will see visions.

through the outpouring of the Holy Spirit on all flesh illustrates that repentance and obedience are enduring prerequisites for revival and receiving God's blessings. Joel's call encourages every believer to earnestly seek a personal and communal revival through sincere repentance, highlighting that pivotal transformations begin with a humble and contrite heart.

**Personal Notes:**

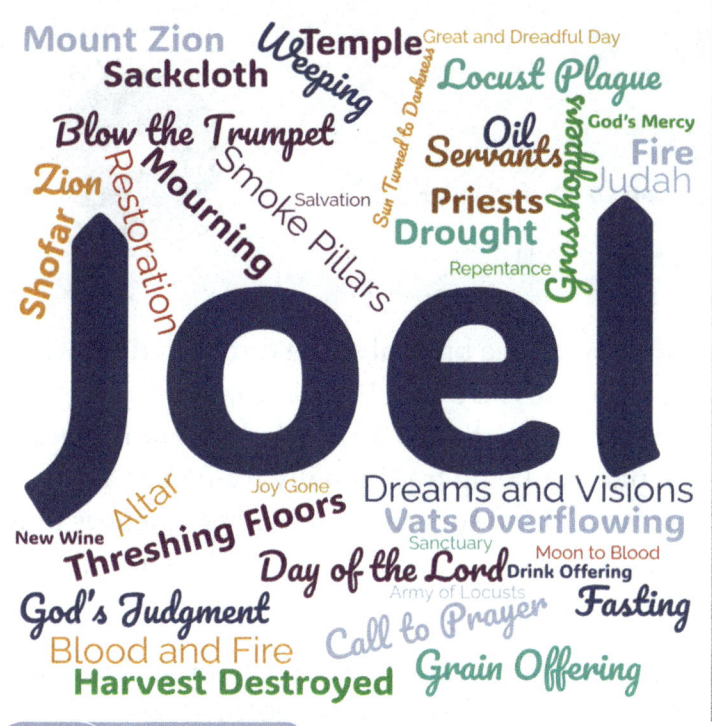

# Reflections on Joel
*Locusts and Restoration*

Temporary, historical judgments act as a summons to repentance. They underscore the importance of turning back in penance before the ultimate day of divine reckoning. For those who respond to this call and repent, God guarantees salvation from judgment and grants them the promise of eternal blessings.

## NOTABLE & POPULAR

**People**

Joel

**Places**

Judah

**Events**

Locust Plague,
Day of the Lord Prophecies

**Verses**

**Joel 1:4** What the devouring locust has left, the swarming locust has eaten; what the swarming locust has left, the young locust has eaten; and what the young locust has left, the destroying locust has eaten.

**Joel 2:25** I will repay you for the years eaten by locusts— the swarming locust, the young locust, the destroying locust, and the devouring locust — My great army that I sent against you.

**Joel 3:10** Beat your plowshares into swords and your pruning hooks into spears. Let the weak say, 'I am strong!'

75

# AMOS

**Author:** Amos

**Time Written:** Likely between 760 and 753 B.C.

**Time Covered:** Around 766 B.C.

*Minor Prophets — Books 28 - 39*

*Amos — Old Testament*

Amos, a simple shepherd from Tekoa, emerged powerfully on the biblical scene during a time when Israel was flourishing economically but deteriorating spiritually. Despite Israel's apparent prosperity, with booming business and expanding borders, beneath the surface lay rampant greed and injustice. Amos was uniquely called by God—despite not being traditionally trained as a prophet—to speak fiercely against the nation's hypocrisy and the superficial religious practices that masked their true spiritual bankruptcy. His harsh admonishments aimed to awaken Israel from its complacency and urge a return to genuine worship and justice. At the heart of Amos's prophecy

**A Key Verse:** Amos 5:14, Seek good, not evil, so that you may live. And the Lord, the God of Hosts, will be with you, as you have claimed.

was a stark warning: the security and prosperity that Israel enjoyed were perilous illusions. The kingdom, engrossed in hypocritical rituals and indifferent to God's truth, was teetering on the brink of divine retribution. Amos's role as a "Burden-bearer," reflected in the Hebrew meaning of his name, was to carry the heavy message of impending judgment due to the people's spiritual indifference and idolatry. His outspoken critiques and vivid imagery, such as visions of famine and destruction, were designed to jolt the people of Israel into recognizing their moral and spiritual failings. The teachings of Amos are a timeless reminder of the danger of complacency in spiritual

**A Popular Verse:** Amos 5:24, But let justice roll on like a river, and righteousness like an ever-flowing stream.

matters. He challenges all believers to examine the depth of their faith and the authenticity of their worship. The prophet's call to repentance emphasizes that true security and prosperity can only come from a steadfast commitment to God's principles. As Amos's message reverberated through Israel, it continues to resonate today, urging us to eschew superficiality in our spiritual practices and to embrace a life of true righteousness and justice.

**Personal Notes:**

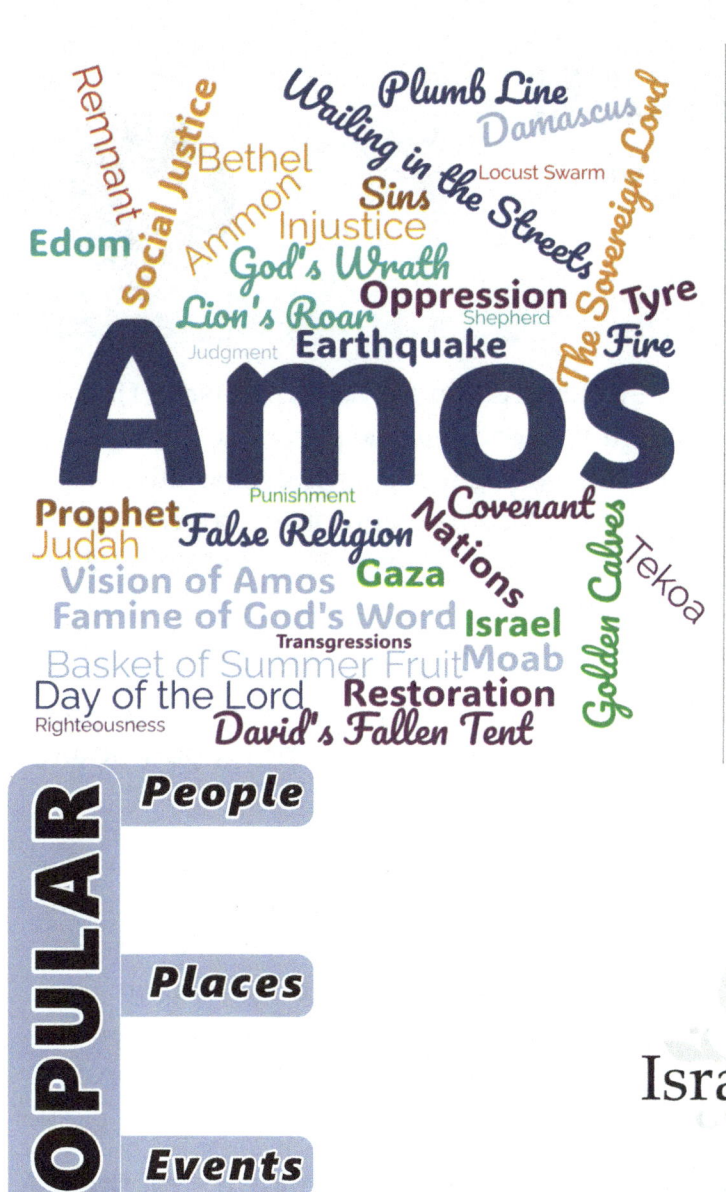

## Reflections on Amos
*Justice and Judgment*

Judgment for wicked deeds was not limited to gentile nations. Israel and Judah were also subject to the wrath of Assyrian aggression due to their transgressions. God's irrefutable case against Israel led to substantial turmoil, evidenced by natural disasters and war. Amos' visions confirmed the prophecy of Samaria's destruction at the hands of Assyrian forces. Despite facing judgment along with other nations, post-exile, Israel and Judah were destined for a position of prominence above their gentile contemporaries.

## NOTABLE & POPULAR

**People**

Amos

**Places**

Israel, Judah

**Events**

Prophecies Against Nations, Visions of Judgment

**Verses**

**Amos 2:4** This is what the Lord says: "For three transgressions of Judah, even four, I will not revoke My judgment, because they reject the Law of the Lord and fail to keep His statutes; they are led astray by the lies in which their fathers walked.

**Amos 3:7** Surely the Lord GOD does nothing without revealing His plan to His servants the prophets.

**Amos 5:24** But let justice roll on like a river, and righteousness like an ever-flowing stream.

**Amos 9:14** I will restore My people Israel from captivity; they will rebuild and inhabit the ruined cities. They will plant vineyards and drink their wine; they will make gardens and eat their fruit.

# OBADIAH

**Author:** Obadiah

**Time Written:** Uncertain. Either Around 840 B.C. or 586 B.C.

**Time Covered:** Around 853 B.C.

The ancient rivalry between brothers Jacob and Esau, key patriarchs in the lineage of Israel (Jacob's descendants) and Edom (Esau's descendants), finds a significant echo in the prophetic utterances of Obadiah. From their prenatal struggles to the hostilities between their progeny, the narrative extends into a deeper illustration of conflict and divine justice. Obadiah's prophecy, concise yet potent, directly addresses the Edomites' perennial antagonism toward Israel. He reproaches Edom for their harsh refusal to assist their kindred nation, highlighting instances from Israel's difficult trek in the wilderness to the catastrophic period of the Babylonian siege. Obadiah's charges against

**A Key Verse:** Obadiah 1:4, Though you soar like the eagle and make your nest among the stars, even from there I will bring you down," declares the Lord.

Edom are severe, underlining a betrayal steeped in pride and a misplaced sense of superiority. As Obadiah unfolds his prophecy, he not only catalogs Edom's offenses but also announces their dire consequences. Edom's delight in Israel's misfortune and their consequent inaction would not go unpunished; total destruction was forecast for them, contrasting sharply with the restoration promised to Israel. This restoration symbolizes not merely a return to their land but a renewal of their covenant place of prominence under God's caring watch. Obadiah's message is rooted in a broader biblical theme of divine justice—God's commitment to right wrongs and defend His people

**A Popular Verse:** Obadiah 1:15, For the Day of the Lord is near for all the nations. As you have done, it will be done to you; your recompense will return upon your own head.

against their adversaries. Understanding Obadiah's prophecy encourages Christians today to reflect on the importance of solidarity and support within the community of faith. It warns against the dangers of pride and the abandonment of kinship, urging a proactive stance in aiding and uplifting one another during trials. It also reassures believers of God's vigilant oversight and His ultimate justice—serving as a reminder that God is not just a spectator but an active participant in the history and lives of His people, rewarding those who are faithful and bringing retribution to those who stand against them.

**Personal Notes:**

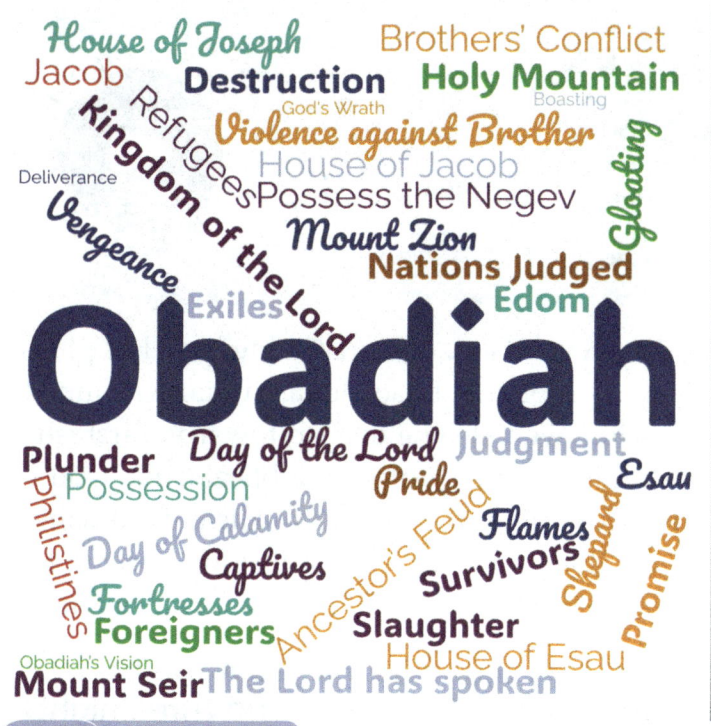

## Reflections on Obadiah
*Edom's Fall*

In times of distress, God's tender care surrounds His people. He issues warnings before delivering judgment on those who oppress them. Victory is assured for His people, showcasing His steadfast support. Ultimately, His faithful followers are destined to inherit the fullness of the Kingdom of God.

## NOTABLE & POPULAR

**People**

**Places**

**Events**

**Verses**

# Obadiah

# Edom

# Prophecy Against Edom

**Obadiah 1:3** The pride of your heart has deceived you, O dwellers in the clefts of the rocks whose habitation is the heights, who say in your heart, 'Who can bring me down to the ground?''

**Obadiah 1:10** Because of the violence against your brother Jacob, you will be covered with shame and cut off forever.

**Obadiah 1:12** But you should not gloat in that day, your brother's day of misfortune, nor rejoice over the people of Judah in the day of their destruction, nor boast proudly in the day of their distress.

# JONAH

**Author:** Jonah

**Time Written:** Likely between 793 and 758 B.C.

**Time Covered:** Around 760 B.C.

Jonah's story is a poignant depiction of the might and mercy of God, demonstrating how His plans persist despite human resistance. Known for his role as a prophet in Israel, Jonah initially shunned his divine calling to preach repentance to the infamous Nineveh, fleeing instead towards Tarshish. His remarkable journey from rebellion to compliance underscores a profound biblical truth: God's will is unstoppable, and He employs extraordinary measures to guide us back to His path. Jonah's reluctance was deeply rooted in his knowledge of God's character—merciful and slow to anger. He feared that the wicked city of Nineveh, if given the chance to repent, would indeed turn from their

**A Key Verse:** Jonah 1:17, Now the Lord had appointed a great fish to swallow Jonah, and Jonah spent three days and three nights in the belly of the fish.

sins and receive God's mercy, a prospect that Jonah begrudgingly hoped to avoid due to his disdain for the Assyrians. God, however, intervened dramatically in Jonah's flight through the ordeal of the storm and the great fish, showcasing His sovereignty and patience. These events led Jonah to reconsider and obey God's command, eventually going to Nineveh and delivering the warning of impending judgment. Contrary to Jonah's personal desires, the people of Nineveh responded with an unexpectedly sincere repentance. This mass transformation was a direct result of God's grace, which Jonah himself struggled to accept, reflecting the sometimes challenging nature of divine

**A Popular Verse:** Jonah 2:2, saying: "In my distress I called to the Lord, and He answered me. From the belly of Sheol I called for help, and You heard my voice.

compassion that extends even to those we might deem undeserving. The narrative of Jonah serves as a vivid lesson on obedience and God's boundless grace. It teaches that God's love and salvation are offered universally—an invitation to all humanity, regardless of past iniquities. This message, authenticated by Jesus Christ according to the Gospel of Matthew, calls us to lay aside our prejudices and embrace God's will, trusting in His greater plan for redemption and reconciliation. The story of Jonah encourages believers to respond to God's call with immediate obedience and to celebrate His mercy, understanding that His saving grace is expansive and not limited to boundaries set by human biases.

**Personal Notes:**

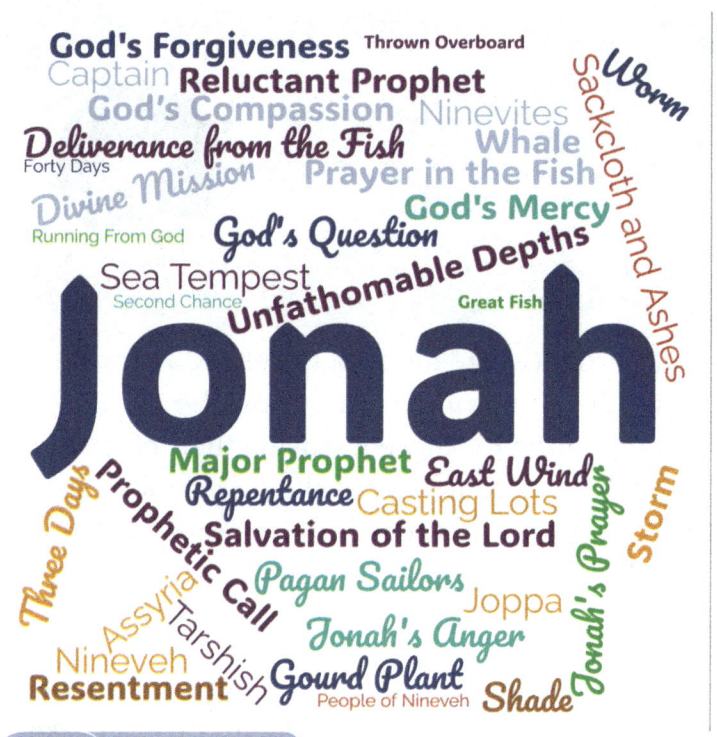

## Reflections on Jonah
*Mercy and Mission*

God calls His people to advocate for repentance among the nations. If they fail to share God's mercy with these nations, they risk incurring His displeasure. God experiences righteous joy when He extends mercy to Gentiles who repent.

## NOTABLE & POPULAR

**People**

Jonah, Ninevites

**Places**

Nineveh, Tarshish

**Events**

Jonah's Flight, Nineveh's Repentance

**Verses**

**Jonah 1:3** Jonah, however, got up to flee to Tarshish, away from the presence of the Lord. He went down to Joppa and found a ship bound for Tarshish. So he paid the fare and went aboard to sail for Tarshish, away from the presence of the Lord.

**Jonah 3:10** When God saw their actions—that they had turned from their evil ways—He relented from the disaster He had threatened to bring upon them.

**Jonah 4:2** So he prayed to the Lord, saying, "O Lord, is this not what I said while I was still in my own country? This is why I was so quick to flee toward Tarshish. I knew that You are a gracious and compassionate God, slow to anger, abounding in loving devotion—One who relents from sending disaster.

# MICAH

**Author:** Micah

**Time Written:** Likely between 735 and 700 B.C.

**Time Covered:** Around 735 B.C.

Micah, hailing from Moresheth, was a prophet with a stern message for both Israel and Judah. Alarmed by the flagrant injustices committed by the wealthy and influential against the impoverished, his prophecies brimmed with divine indignation for those misusing their positions for personal advantage. Micah's teachings reflect an unyielding principle: God's expectation for His people to lead lives imbued with justice, mercy, and humility, as outlined in the evocative call of Micah 6:8. This clarion summons to live righteously underscores the timeless relevance of Micah's message, highlighting that the demonstration of one's faith is intrinsically linked to acts of justice

**A Key Verse:** Micah 5:2, But you, Bethlehem Ephrathah, who are small among the clans of Judah, out of you will come forth for Me One to be ruler over Israel — One whose origins are of old, from the days of eternity.

and compassion. Beyond his rebukes, Micah was also a prophet of hope, foretelling the advent of the Messiah and envisioning a future era of peace and devotion to God. His prophecy in Micah 5:2—pointing to Bethlehem as the birthplace of a ruler "whose goings forth are from of old, from everlasting"—is a cornerstone of messianic anticipation celebrated especially during the Christmas season. This prophetic vision speaks to a profound truth about God's redemptive plans for humanity, extending beyond immediate judgment to a future filled with restoration and peace under the just rule of the Messiah. Micah's dual themes of imminent judgment and future hope

**A Popular Verse:** Micah 6:8, He has shown you, O man, what is good. And what does the Lord require of you but to act justly, to love mercy, and to walk humbly with your God?

offer a powerful reminder to all believers about the seriousness with which God views justice and righteousness. They also affirm His unwavering commitment to His covenant, promising that despite the people's failures, He will not forsake them but will instead send a Deliverer to restore and rule. Consequently, Micah's message encourages us to reflect deeply on our own lives, urging us to align our actions with God's mandates of justice and mercy while holding firmly to the hope of Christ's ultimate rule and redemption.

**Personal Notes:**

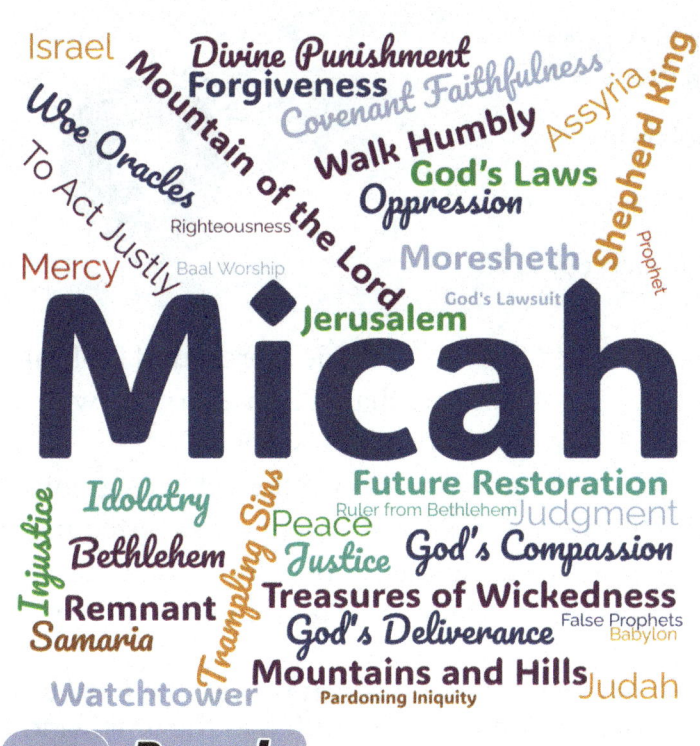

## Reflections on Micah
*Judgment and Hope*

Impending judgment was foretold for Samaria and Judah due to their blatant violations of the covenant. A call for repentance was issued, serving as a potential means to delay or avert the judgment. God reaffirmed His commitment to His people with promises of restoration from defeat and exile. Blessings of victory, growth, and peace were promised to His renewed people.

## NOTABLE & POPULAR

**People**

Micah

**Places**

Judah, Israel

**Events**

Prophecies of Judgment and Restoration

**Verses**

**Micah 1:2** Hear, O peoples, all of you; listen, O earth, and everyone in it! May the Lord GOD bear witness against you, the Lord from His holy temple.

**Micah 7:7** But as for me, I will look to the Lord; I will wait for the God of my salvation. My God will hear me.

**Micah 7:18-19** Who is a God like You, who pardons iniquity and passes over the transgression of the remnant of His inheritance— who does not retain His anger forever, because He delights in loving devotion? He will again have compassion on us; He will vanquish our iniquities. You will cast out all our sins into the depths of the sea.

# NAHUM

**Author:** Nahum

**Time Written:** Likely between 663 and 612 B.C.

**Time Covered:** Around 697 B.C.

The stories of Jonah and Nahum, concerning the great city of Nineveh, provide a profound biblical narrative on the themes of divine mercy and judgment. Jesus's teaching that "From everyone who has been given much, much will be required" (Luke 12:48) aptly encapsulates Nineveh's experiences across these accounts. Initially, under Jonah's reluctant prophecy, Nineveh was granted an extraordinary opportunity to know the true God. The city's widespread repentance averted the destruction God had planned, showcasing His willingness to withhold judgment in the face of genuine contrition. However, a century later, the scenario dramatically shifted as depicted in the

**A Key Verse:** Nahum 1:3, The Lord is slow to anger and great in power; the Lord will by no means leave the guilty unpunished. His path is in the whirlwind and storm, and clouds are the dust beneath His feet.

book of Nahum. The Ninevites, once recipients of divine mercy, reverted to their former violent and idolatrous ways, demonstrating a forgetfulness of the grace once extended to them. Nahum's prophecy, therefore, marks a stark contrast to Jonah's, as he foretells the inevitable downfall of Nineveh due to its return to wicked practices. This time, there would be no reprieve, and the prophecy of Nahum came to pass with devastating accuracy—the mighty city was so completely destroyed by the Babylonians that its location was lost to history until modern archaeological discoveries. The juxtaposition of these prophetic books highlights a critical spiritual truth: God's

**A Popular Verse:** Nahum 1:7, The Lord is good, a stronghold in the day of distress; He cares for those who trust in Him.

mercy is profound, but it is accompanied by a call to sustained obedience and transformation. Nahum, whose name signifies comfort and consolation, ironically announces a message of destruction—but it is a message that would have brought solace to those oppressed by Assyrian cruelty. This narrative teaches that while God is slow to anger and abundant in mercy, His justice is equally stringent, and He holds individuals and nations accountable for the privileges of divine revelation they receive. In this context, Nahum can be seen as a sequel to Jonah, emphasizing that the mercy God extends is not a license for complacency but a call to a changed life—a theme that resonates with the responsibility and accountability of those who receive much from God.

**Personal Notes:**

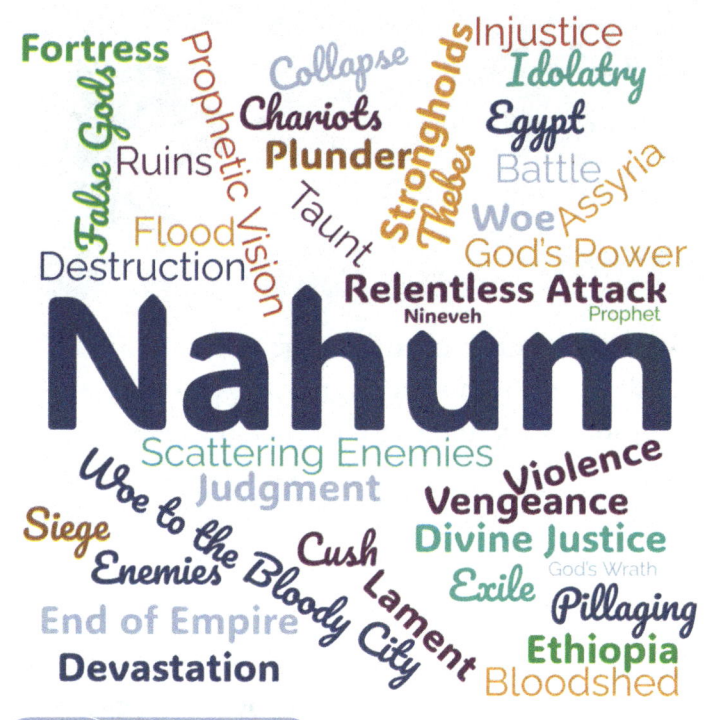

## Reflections on Nahum
*Nineveh's Fall*

God's divine justice and judgment are worthy of exaltation. Nineveh and other nations guilty of harming His people would face the ordeal of judgment. God's protective hand would safeguard His faithful, restoring them from the depths of destruction and exile.

## NOTABLE & POPULAR

**People**

Nahum

**Places**

Nineveh

**Events**

Prediction of Nineveh's Downfall

**Verses**

**Nahum 1:15** Look to the mountains— the feet of one who brings good news, who proclaims peace! Celebrate your feasts, O Judah; fulfill your vows. For the wicked will never again march through you; they will be utterly cut off.

**Nahum 2:13** "Behold, I am against you," declares the Lord of Hosts. "I will send your chariots up in smoke, and the sword will devour your young lions. I will cut off your prey from the earth, and the voices of your messengers will no longer be heard."

**Nahum 3:19** There is no healing for your injury; your wound is severe. All who hear the news of you applaud your downfall, for who has not experienced your constant cruelty?

# HABAKKUK

**Author:** Habakkuk

**Time Written:** Likely between 610 and 605 B.C.

**Time Covered:** Around 625 B.C.

Amidst the tumultuous days leading up to the Babylonian conquest of Judah, the prophet Habakkuk grappled with difficult questions about God's justice and sovereignty. As he observed the moral decay of his society and the stubbornness of Judah in refusing to heed God's calls to repentance, Habakkuk turned to God in perplexity. The Lord's response—that He would employ the even more corrupt Babylonians as agents of correction—initially bewildered the prophet. This revelation challenged Habakkuk's understanding of divine justice, propelling him into deeper theological reflection and prayer, where he sought clarity on how a holy God could use a wicked

**A Key Verse:** Habakkuk 1:5, "Look at the nations and observe— be utterly astounded! For I am doing a work in your days that you would never believe even if someone told you.

nation for His redemptive purposes. Habakkuk's journey of faith underscores a profound biblical principle: the righteous will live by faith (Habakkuk 2:4). This principle is central not only to understanding God's dealings with nations but also in personal spiritual growth. Facing the apparent paradox of God's methods, Habakkuk chose to trust in God's perfect wisdom and timing. He recognized that God's ways might not always align with human expectations but they are always grounded in ultimate good. This act of faith is remarkably expressed towards the end of his book, where despite the looming catastrophe, he praises God's sovereignty and commits to

**A Popular Verse:** Habakkuk 2:4, Look at the proud one; his soul is not upright — but the righteous will live by faith —

rejoicing in the Lord, regardless of external circumstances. For contemporary Christians, the Prophet's response offers a vital lesson in faithfulness and trust in God. When faced with situations that seem unjust or beyond our understanding, we are invited to embrace, as Habakkuk did, a posture of trust and dependency on God. His story encourages us to hold onto God's promises and character, especially when the reasons behind His actions are not immediately evident. In learning to rely on God's wisdom and timing, we can navigate life's uncertainties with confidence and peace, knowing that all history is held in His capable hands. This challenges us to live by faith, cling to God's truths, and trust in His eternal plan, cultivating a faith that endures through all trials.

**Personal Notes:**

# Reflections on Habakkuk
*Questioning Faith*

God's patience has limits when confronted with persistent and grave sin among His people. He may use wicked non-believers as instruments of chastisement against His own. Believers are encouraged to candidly acknowledge their struggles before God. Additionally, they must deepen their faith and learn to rely on God, particularly during difficult times.

## NOTABLE & POPULAR

**People**

Habakkuk

**Places**

Judah

**Events**

Dialogues with God, Vision of Judgment

**Verses**

**Habakkuk 1:2** How long, O Lord, must I call for help but You do not hear, or cry out to You, "Violence!" but You do not save?

**Habakkuk 1:12** Are You not from everlasting, O Lord, my God, my Holy One? We will not die. O Lord, You have appointed them to execute judgment; O Rock, You have established them for correction.

**Habakkuk 3:2** O Lord, I have heard the report of You; I stand in awe, O Lord, of Your deeds. Revive them in these years; make them known in these years. In Your wrath, remember mercy!

**Habakkuk 3:19** GOD the Lord is my strength; He makes my feet like those of a deer; He makes me walk upon the heights! For the choirmaster. With stringed instruments.

# ZEPHANIAH

**Author:** Zephaniah

**Time Written:** Likely between 635 and 625 B.C.

**Time Covered:** Around 638 B.C.

Zephaniah's ministry emerged during a pivotal era of Judah's history, marked by both spiritual and political upheaval. His prophetic voice was one of the influences that spurred the reforms under King Josiah. However, despite outward changes, the reform failed to eradicate the deep-seated corruption within the nation. Zephaniah's prophecies deliver a stark message: the day of the Lord—a time of profound judgment and correction—is imminent. This day would sweep through Judah and its neighboring nations, addressing the entrenched sin with God's just wrath. However, Zephaniah also proclaims a message of hope—after the period of judgment, God promises

**A Key Verse:** Zephaniah 1:18, Neither their silver nor their gold will be able to deliver them on the Day of the Lord's wrath. The whole earth will be consumed by the fire of His jealousy." For indeed, He will make a sudden end of all who dwell on the earth.

restoration and blessings through the coming of the Messiah. This duality reflects the profound nature of God's interaction with His people, balancing between divine justice and mercy. The name Zephaniah, which means "Yahweh hides" or "Yahweh has hidden," is quite telling of his times and personal circumstances. Likely born in the reign of the notoriously wicked King Manasseh, his name might suggest divine protection from the king's brutal policies. His prophecies showcase a deep understanding of societal structures and political dynamics, hinting at his possible connections to the royal family. This background equipped him to speak authoritatively to the

**A Popular Verse:** Zephaniah 3:17, The Lord your God is among you; He is mighty to save. He will rejoice over you with gladness; He will quiet you with His love; He will rejoice over you with singing."

spiritual and societal issues of his day, making his message particularly resonant and effective. In today's context, Zephaniah's teachings serve as a reminder of God's "goodness and severity." Sin is never trivialized or overlooked by God, and His justice will inevitably address it. However, His promise to never forsake His covenant people offers a profound comfort and hope. For believers, Zephaniah's life and prophecies encourage a balanced view of God's character—one that does not diminish His righteousness in the face of sin or His mercy in times of repentance. As we navigate our faith journey, Zephaniah inspires us to embrace both the severity and the goodness of God, leading us towards a more holistic and reverent relationship with Him.

**Personal Notes:**

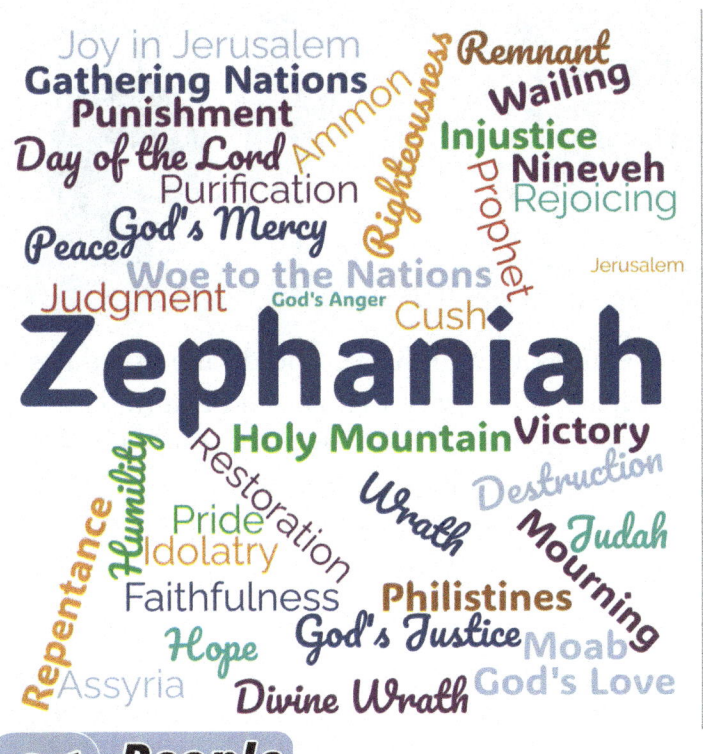

# Reflections on Zephaniah
*Day of the Lord*

God used the Babylonians as instruments of severe judgment against Judah and many other nations in response to their transgressions. Safety is found in the humble pursuit of God, offering a shield against harm. The downfall of other nations would ultimately bring benefit to Israel. After God's judgment has been fulfilled, His plan is to purify both Gentiles and Jews, bestowing abundant blessings upon them.

## NOTABLE & POPULAR

**People**

Zephaniah

**Places**

Judah

**Events**

Day of the Lord Prophecies

**Verses**

**Zephaniah 1:14** The great Day of the Lord is near— near and coming quickly. Listen, the Day of the Lord! Then the cry of the mighty will be bitter.

**Zephaniah 2:3** Seek the Lord, all you humble of the earth who carry out His justice. Seek righteousness; seek humility. Perhaps you will be sheltered on the day of the Lord's anger.

**Zephaniah 2:13** And He will stretch out His hand against the north and destroy Assyria; He will make Nineveh a desolation, as dry as a desert.

**Zephaniah 3:20** At that time I will bring you in; yes, at that time I will gather you. For I will give you fame and praise among all the peoples of the earth when I restore your captives before your very eyes," says the Lord.

# HAGGAI

**Author:** Haggai

**Time Written:** Around 520 B.C.

**Time Covered:** Around 520 B.C.

Sixteen years after the Jews returned from Babylonian exile with high hopes and divine mandates to rebuild the temple, their initial zeal had fizzled out amidst everyday challenges and external opposition. As the construction of the temple lagged due to personal distractions and resistance from adversaries, the spiritual fervor that once ignited their hearts had significantly waned. Recognizing the critical juncture at which the people stood, the prophet Haggai stepped forward with urgent and compelling messages to reignite their commitment. He not merely urged but exhorted the people to rise above their complacency, emphasizing the importance of courage, faith,

**A Key Verse:** Haggai 1:9, You expected much, but behold, it amounted to little. And what you brought home, I blew away. Why? declares the Lord of Hosts. Because My house still lies in ruins, while each of you is busy with his own house.

and holiness in rejuvenating their divine assignment. Haggai's own name, potentially meaning "festive" or related to "festival," perhaps indicating his birth during a significant religious feast, underscores the celebratory hope his prophecies aimed to restore. This connection to festivity is fitting as his prophetic ministry sought to reawaken a communal spirit centered on worship and devotion through the temple's restoration. His messages came at a pivotal time, especially during the Feast of Tabernacles—a time recalling God's past provision and protection. It was this season that Haggai chose to deliver a powerful reminder of God's continued faithfulness and the blessed

**A Popular Verse:** Haggai 2:9, The latter glory of this house will be greater than the former, says the Lord of Hosts. And in this place I will provide peace, declares the Lord of Hosts."

outcomes of obediently prioritizing His work. The impact of Haggai's stern yet inspiring calls was profound. Leaders like Zerubbabel and Joshua the high priest, alongside the broader community, were spurred into action, resuming the work with renewed vigor. Under their collective efforts, the temple's construction progressed, reflecting a revitalized commitment to God's mandate. For believers today, Haggai's example teaches the importance of prioritizing divine purposes over personal agendas. His life and messages remind us that when God's people align their efforts with His will and work diligently towards His goals, they not only fulfill their calling but also position themselves to receive the blessings God promises to those who obey and serve Him faithfully.

**Personal Notes:**

## Reflections on Haggai
*Temple Rebuilding*

The initial group of returnees from exile experienced an outpouring of God's blessings. In God's Kingdom, His priorities must take precedence over personal comforts. It's crucial for those serving in God's Kingdom to remain pure. The hope of God's people is centered on the Temple and the house of David, ultimately realized in the coming of Christ. Through Christ, God's people are destined to inherit the earth.

## NOTABLE & POPULAR

**People**

Haggai, Zerubbabel

**Places**

Jerusalem

**Events**

Encouragement to Rebuild the Temple

**Verses**

**Haggai 1:4** "Is it a time for you yourselves to live in your paneled houses, while this house lies in ruins?"

**Haggai 1:5-6** Now this is what the Lord of Hosts says: "Consider carefully your ways. You have planted much but harvested little. You eat but never have enough. You drink but never have your fill. You put on clothes but never get warm. You earn wages to put into a bag pierced through."

**Haggai 1:8** Go up into the hills, bring down lumber, and build the house, so that I may take pleasure in it and be glorified, says the Lord.

**Haggai 2:6** For this is what the Lord of Hosts says: "Once more, in a little while, I will shake the heavens and the earth, the sea and the dry land.

# ZECHARIAH

**Author:** Zechariah

**Time Written:** Likely between 520 and 470 B.C.

**Time Covered:** Around 520 B.C.

As the Jews confronted the daunting task of completing the temple they had started upon their return from Babylonian exile, God raised Zechariah, a prophet and priest, to inspire action and dedication among the people. Zechariah's mission was to energize the community by casting a vision of the temple's significance beyond its immediate construction. He prophesied that this very temple would one day host the manifested glory of the Messiah, an event that would fulfill divine promises and elevate the spiritual and national identity of Israel. Unlike his contemporary Haggai, who sternly rebuked the people for their neglect, Zechariah adopted a more encouraging approach,

**A Key Verse:** Zechariah 9:9, Rejoice greatly, O Daughter of Zion! Shout in triumph, O Daughter of Jerusalem! See, your King comes to you, righteous and victorious, humble and riding on a donkey, on a colt, the foal of a donkey.

focusing on the hopeful future and the critical role of the temple in God's overarching plan. Zechariah's prophecies are richly messianic (things relating to the Messiah), interspersing visions of hope with calls to action. He not only urged completion of the temple but also unfolded the future events that would transpire around it, including the Messiah's triumphant entry into Jerusalem and pivotal moments leading to His crucifixion. These prophecies served to remind the people that their labor was not just for a building but was tied to the very fulfillment of God's promises throughout history. This perspective was intended to lift their sights beyond the immediate challenges and

**A Popular Verse:** Zechariah 4:6, So he said to me, "This is the word of the Lord to Zerubbabel: Not by might nor by power, but by My Spirit, says the Lord of Hosts.

motivate them with the sacred purpose of their work. The name Zechariah, meaning "Yahweh remembers," perfectly encapsulates the theme of his prophecies. It reassured the people that God had not forgotten the covenant made with their ancestors and that He would faithfully remember His promises regarding their future. This reminder was crucial in rekindling their commitment to finishing the temple, a symbol of God's continuing presence and favor. For believers today, Zechariah's life and ministry emphasize the importance of remembering God's past faithfulness as motivation for current obedience and service. His messages encourage us to engage wholeheartedly in God's work, assured that our efforts are integral to the fulfillment of His divine purposes.

**Personal Notes:**

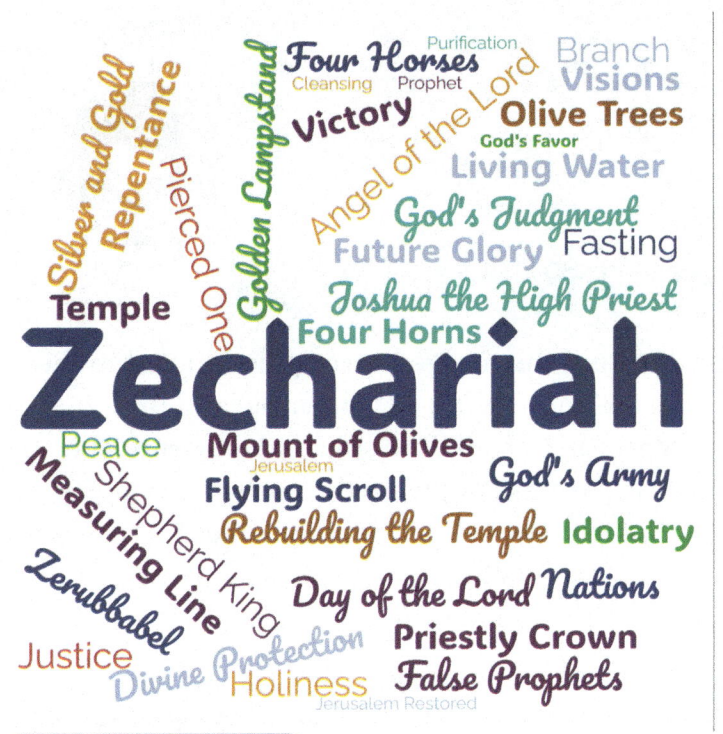

# Reflections on Zechariah
*Future Hope*

After the exile, God lavished His people with splendid blessings through Zerubbabel, a descendant of King David, and along with Joshua, the High Priest (not the same Joshua who wrote the Old Testament book and who was Moses' successor). Despite the failings of the returning exiles, God faithfully upheld His promises. With supreme power to defeat His enemies, God assures a day of decisive victory. The final battle will usher in ultimate triumph for God's people.

## NOTABLE & POPULAR

**People:** Zechariah, Joshua (High Priest)

**Places:** Jerusalem

**Events:** Visions, Messianic Prophecies

**Verses:**

Zechariah 1:3 So tell the people that this is what the Lord of Hosts says: 'Return to Me, declares the Lord of Hosts, and I will return to you, says the Lord of Hosts.'

Zechariah 7:13 And just as I had called and they would not listen, so when they called I would not listen, says the Lord of Hosts.

Zechariah 13:9 This third I will bring through the fire; I will refine them like silver and test them like gold. They will call on My name, and I will answer them. I will say, 'They are My people,' and they will say, 'The Lord is our God.'"

# MALACHI

**Author:** Malachi

**Time Written:** Between 440 and 400 B.C.

**Time Covered:** Around 430 B.C.

Years after their return from exile, the people of Israel found themselves once again tangled in the web of sin that had once led to their captivity. Despite the completion of the temple and previous prophetic encouragements to live in obedience, the community sank into spiritual lethargy. The religious leaders, instead of guiding the flock towards righteousness, were themselves entangled in corrupt practices. In this troubling period, God sent Malachi, meaning "My messenger," to confront and correct His wayward people. As a contemporary of Nehemiah, Malachi addressed issues like corrupt priesthood, unchecked immorality, and a waning hope that dulled their spiritual senses to

> **A Key Verse:** Malachi 3:1, "Behold, I will send My messenger, who will prepare the way before Me. Then the Lord whom you seek will suddenly come to His temple—the Messenger of the covenant, in whom you delight—see, He is coming," says the Lord of Hosts.

the promises God had made through earlier prophets like Haggai and Zechariah. Malachi's prophetic endeavors were punctuated by a dynamic question-and-answer format, which vividly brought to the forefront the people's doubts, hypocrisy, and disobedience. This method not only exposed the depth of their sin but also articulated God's unchanging love and justice. People questioned God's love amidst their hardships, yet Malachi pointed out that their own rebellious actions had barred the blessings they were meant to receive. The stark contrast between their expected state as God's blessed nation and their current reality as a mere Persian province

> **A Popular Verse:** Malachi 3:10, Bring the full tithe into the storehouse, so that there may be food in My house. Test Me in this," says the Lord of Hosts. "See if I will not open the windows of heaven and pour out for you blessing without measure.

amplified their despair, leading to further spiritual numbness and misconduct. By addressing issues like inter-marriages with pagan worshipers of false gods, divorce, and false worship, Malachi wasn't just criticizing; he was calling the people to a profound reformation. His message underscored the need for sincere repentance to pave the way for the Messiah, the promised "Messenger of the covenant." The challenges highlighted by Malachi are emblematic reminders for us even today—remaining faithful and obedient is pivotal in experiencing God's promises and presence. The prophetic voice of Malachi calls believers across ages to reflect and reform, anticipating the ultimate fulfillment of God's redemptive plan through the Messiah.

**Personal Notes:**

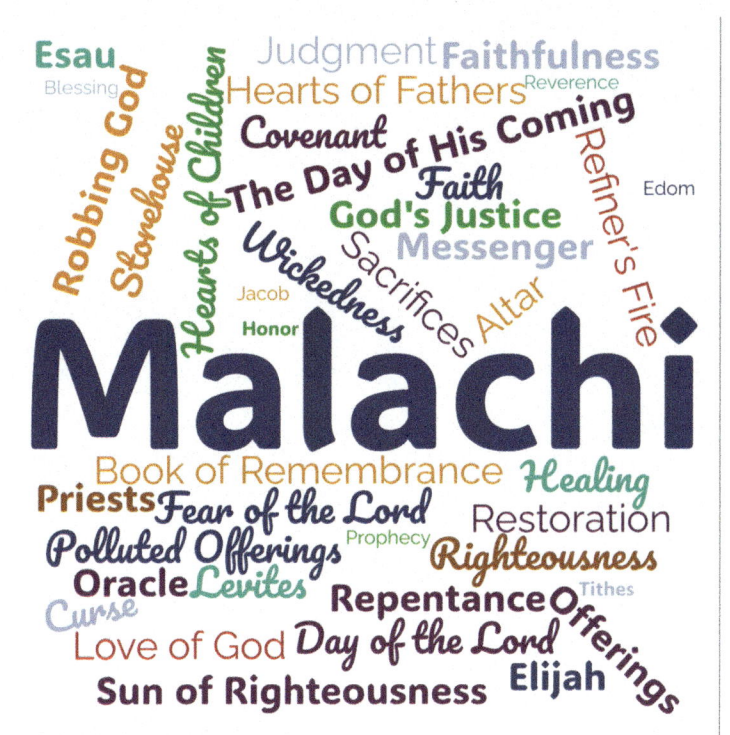

# Reflections on Malachi
*Covenant Faithfulness*

In the closing years of the Old Testament period, the people of Israel were marred by sin. Despite their failings, God extended an offer of forgiveness to His people. He promised that the Messiah would come to purify the nation. A day of reckoning awaits when the wicked will face judgment and the righteous will receive their due reward.

## Notable & Popular

**People:** Malachi

**Places:** Judah

**Events:** Critiques of Priests, Prophecy of Elijah

**Verses:**

**Malachi 1:6** "A son honors his father, and a servant his master. But if I am a father, where is My honor? And if I am a master, where is your fear of Me?" says the Lord of Hosts to you priests who despise My name. "But you ask, 'How have we despised Your name?'

**Malachi 2:10** Do we not all have one Father? Did not one God create us? Why then do we break faith with one another so as to profane the covenant of our fathers?

**Malachi 3:7** Yet from the days of your fathers, you have turned away from My statutes and have not kept them. Return to Me, and I will return to you," says the Lord of Hosts. "But you ask, 'How can we return?'

**Malachi 4:5** Behold, I will send you Elijah the prophet before the coming of the great and awesome Day of the Lord.

# THE GOSPELS and ACTS

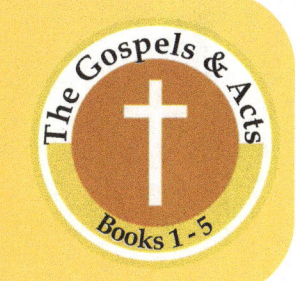

## John   Acts   Mark
## The Gospels and Acts
## Luke   Matthew

The New Testament consists of twenty-seven books, beginning with the four gospels that intricately describe the life of Jesus Christ. Written through the guidance of the Holy Spirit, these gospels by Matthew, Mark, Luke, and John, each provide a unique portrayal of Jesus' life and ministry. Matthew, Mark, and John were apostles closely following Jesus, while Luke, a medical doctor and companion of Paul the apostle, also penned one of these accounts. These books communicate the miraculous deeds, profound teachings, and healing works of Christ, underscoring His divine nature as God incarnate ('in the flesh' or in human form), who came to earth to offer salvation through His sacrificial death and victorious resurrection.

Uniquely, the book of Acts stands as the historical narrative within the New Testament. Distinct from the gospels, Acts focuses on the acts and experiences of the apostles after Jesus' ascension. Authored by Luke, this book details the spread of the gospel starting from Jerusalem and reaching out to Judea, Samaria, and ultimately the wider Roman Empire. It documents the early days of the Christian church, the miraculous work of the Holy Spirit, and the inclusive nature of God's salvation, granted to both Jews and Gentiles. The book culminates with the apostle Paul under house arrest in Rome, actively preaching the gospel.

The central message woven throughout these books is the transformative power of Jesus Christ—God in human flesh—who entered our world to redeem humanity. Through His death and resurrection, He offers forgiveness and eternal life to all who believe. Acts reinforces this message by illustrating the robust growth of the early church and the unwavering commitment of the apostles to spread the hope of the gospel. Theirs work, or 'acts' continues to impact lives today.

**Personal Notes:**

# MATTHEW

**Author:** Matthew

**Time Written:** Likely 55 to 65 A.D.

**Time Covered:** Around 5 B.C. to 30 A.D.

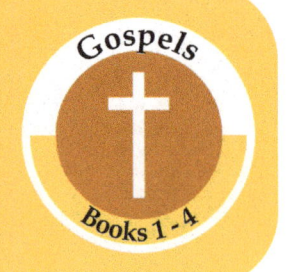

Matthew's Gospel presents Jesus as the King of the Jews, the long-awaited Messiah. Matthew himself, whose name means "Gift of the Lord" and who was also called Levi, was a tax collector called by Jesus to be a disciple. Writing primarily for a Jewish audience, Matthew meticulously documents the life and ministry of Jesus to show that He fulfills the Old Testament prophecies concerning the Messiah. The title, "According to Matthew," suggests the existence of other Gospel accounts during that time, each contributing a unique perspective on the life of Christ. In his Gospel, Matthew includes dozens of Old Testament quotations in order to provide overwhelming

**A Key Verse:** Matthew 5:17, Do not think that I have come to abolish the Law or the Prophets. I have not come to abolish them, but to fulfill them.

evidence that Jesus is the promised Savior. He starts with Jesus' genealogy, linking Him directly to Abraham and David. Then, he chronicles Jesus' baptism, teachings, and miracles, painting a comprehensive picture that conclusively points to Jesus' kingship. Even in the apparent defeat of the Crucifixion, Matthew leads us to the victorious Resurrection, underscoring that the King of the Jews lives and reigns. Matthew's central message is clear: Jesus is the fulfillment of the ancient promises made by God to His people. The word "fulfilled" emerges as a prominent theme throughout, emphasizing Jesus' role in completing God's redemptive work as foretold by the

**A Popular Verse:** Matthew 5:16, In the same way, let your light shine before men, that they may see your good deeds and glorify your Father in heaven.

prophets. The Gospel encourages believers by affirming the continuity of God's plan from the Old Testament to the New, reassuring them that God's promises are steadfast and true, finding their completion in Jesus Christ.

**Personal Notes:**

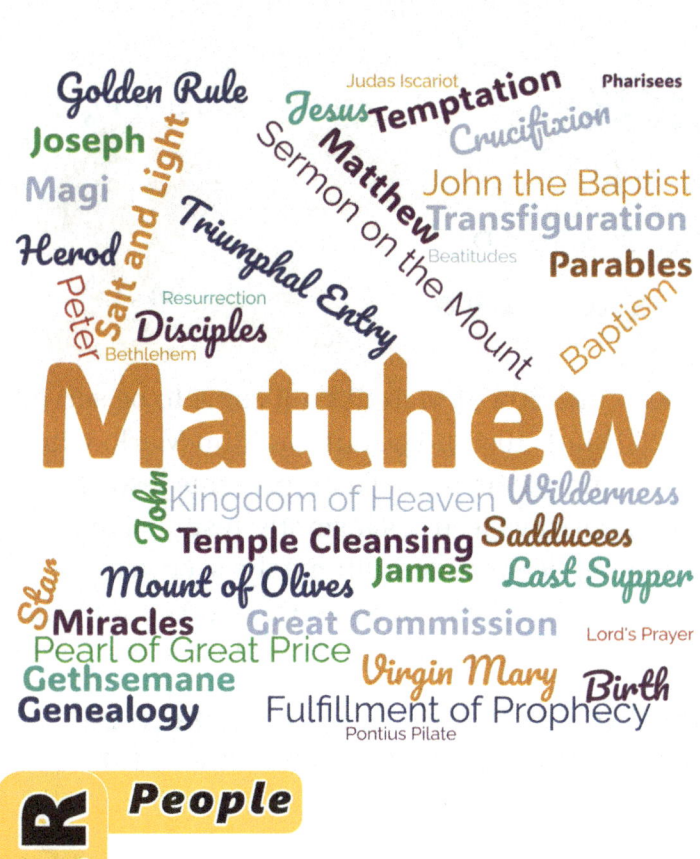

## Reflections on Matthew
*Jesus the Messiah*

Jesus fulfills the Old Testament prophecies, embodying the long-awaited King, or Messiah. He inaugurated God's kingdom on Earth. It is the duty of His followers to spread the message of the Kingdom to all nations. Despite the suffering they may face, they are comforted by the assurance of Jesus' constant presence. With His triumphant return, Jesus will bring about the consummation of God's Kingdom.

## NOTABLE & POPULAR

**People**

Jesus, Mary, Joseph, John the Baptist

**Places**

Bethlehem, Nazareth, Galilee, Jerusalem

**Events**

Birth of Jesus, Sermon on the Mount, Parables, Crucifixion, Resurrection

**Verses**

**Matthew 5:43-44** You have heard that it was said, 'Love your neighbor' and 'Hate your enemy.' But I tell you, love your enemies and pray for those who persecute you,

**Matthew 6:9-13** So then, this is how you should pray: 'Our Father in heaven, hallowed be Your name. Your kingdom come, Your will be done, on earth as it is in heaven. Give us this day our daily bread. And forgive us our debts, as we also have forgiven our debtors. And lead us not into temptation, but deliver us from the evil one.'

**Matthew 16:26** What will it profit a man if he gains the whole world, yet forfeits his soul? Or what can a man give in exchange for his soul?

**Matthew 27:31** After they had mocked Him, they removed the robe and put His own clothes back on Him. Then they led Him away to crucify Him.

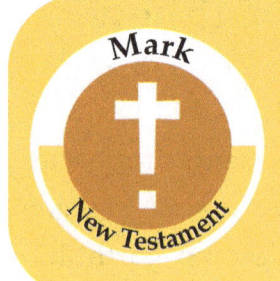

# MARK

**Author:** Mark

**Time Written:** Likely 55 to 59 A.D.

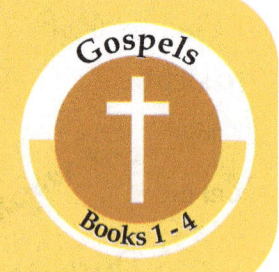

**Time Covered:** Around 5 B.C. to 30 A.D.

Mark's Gospel encapsulates its essence in a single verse: "the Son of Man did not come to be served, but to serve, and to give His life as a ransom for many" (Mark 10:45). The author, John Mark, who was closely associated with the apostles Paul, Barnabas, and particularly Peter, presents Jesus as a tireless Servant. By focusing on action, Mark's narrative portrays Jesus as instantly responsive to His Father's will, dedicating His life to preaching, teaching, healing, and ultimately, sacrificing Himself for humanity. Mark's account, known from its ancient title Kata Markon, stands out for its brisk pace and sense of urgency. Mark's Gospel, considered the earliest written, is distinctive for its

> **A Key Verse:** Mark 10:45, For even the Son of Man did not come to be served, but to serve, and to give His life as a ransom for many."

brevity and immediacy. Unlike the other Gospels, Mark omits detailed genealogies, the virgin birth, and even the "Sermon on the Mount." Instead, he centers on Jesus' dynamic ministry, using the term "immediately" frequently to convey a sense of swift movement and decisive action. He also includes very few Old Testament quotations, suggesting his primary audience was first-century Greek and Roman Christians. The inclusion of occasional Aramaic terms, which Mark thoughtfully translates, indicates his care for clarity and understanding for his readers. The heart of Mark's message revolves around service and sacrifice, highlighting Jesus Christ as the dedicated Servant

> **A Popular Verse:** Mark 12:30-31, Love the Lord your God with all your heart and with all your soul and with all your mind and with all your strength.' The second is this: 'Love your neighbor as yourself.' No other commandment is greater than these."

and Savior of the world. Through the chapters, we witness Jesus' relentless ministry to others, culminating in His ultimate sacrifice on the cross. Post-resurrection, Jesus commissions His disciples to carry forward His work, imbued with His power and example. Mark's portrayal serves as an enduring reminder to all believers to pursue a life of humble service and steadfast faith, walking in the footsteps of the perfect Servant.

**Personal Notes:**

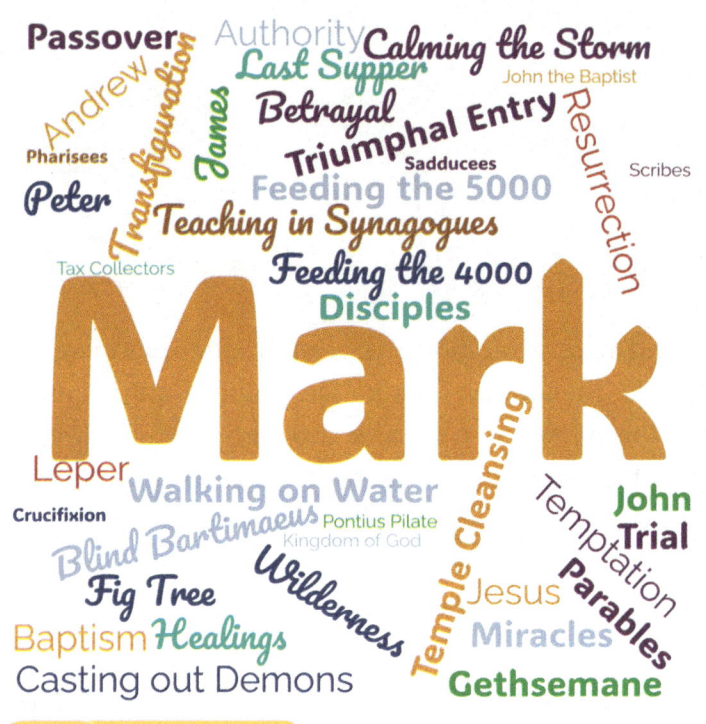

# Reflections on Mark
*Suffering Servant*

Jesus emerged as the long-awaited Messiah for Israel. His revelation to His twelve disciples was unique and intimate, affirming His divine identity as the Son of God. Though He shunned public acclaim, He bravely chose to suffer and die for His people. He also showed a profound commitment to offering salvation to the Gentiles. Spreading the Good News about Jesus wields transformative power against evil forces.

## NOTABLE & POPULAR

**People**

Jesus, Peter, James, John, Judas Iscariot

**Places**

Galilee, Judea, Gethsemane, Golgotha

**Events**

Baptism of Jesus, Miracles, Teachings, Transfiguration, Crucifixion, Resurrection

**Verses**

Mark 1:17 "Come, follow Me," Jesus said, "and I will make you fishers of men."

Mark 10:14-15 But when Jesus saw this, He was indignant and told them, "Let the little children come to Me, and do not hinder them! For the kingdom of God belongs to such as these. Truly I tell you, anyone who does not receive the kingdom of God like a little child will never enter it."

Mark 12:33 and to love Him with all your heart and with all your understanding and with all your strength, and to love your neighbor as yourself, which is more important than all burnt offerings and sacrifices."

Mark 16:6 But he said to them, "Do not be alarmed. You are looking for Jesus the Nazarene, who was crucified. He has risen! He is not here! See the place where they put Him.

# LUKE

**Author:** Luke

**Time Written:** Likely 58 to 65 A.D.

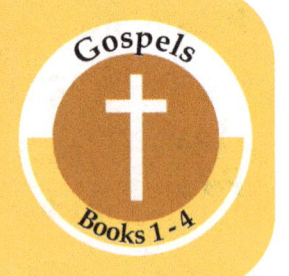

**Time Covered:** Around 6 B.C. to 30 A.D.

Luke, a physician by trade, brings a compassionate and warm touch to his Gospel, documenting the perfect humanity of Jesus Christ, the Son of Man. Unlike the apostles, Luke was neither an original disciple nor an eyewitness to Jesus' ministry. Believed to have come to faith through the teachings of the apostle Paul, Luke accompanied Paul on some of his missionary journeys. Unique among New Testament authors for being a Gentile convert, Luke's perspective offers a universal appeal, reflected in his detailed account of Jesus' ancestry, birth, and early life, leading methodically into His ministry. Luke's Gospel stands out for its rich use of parables and unique miracles. Of the

**A Key Verse:** Luke 19:10, For the Son of Man came to seek and to save the lost."

twenty-five parables included, seventeen are exclusive to Luke. Similarly, he describes seven miracles not documented in the other Synoptic Gospels (or the Gospels of Matthew, Mark, and Luke which have many of the same stories and similar sequences- all in contrast to the Gospel of John which is more distinct). Luke's narrative is filled with details that provide a fuller picture of Jesus' life, such as the angelic announcement to Mary and the birth of John the Baptist, as well as a rare glimpse into Jesus' boyhood. These elements, along with the compassionate portrayal of Jesus, offer readers a deeply human and relatable portrait of the Savior. At the heart of Luke's Gospel is

**A Popular Verse:** Luke 6:31, Do to others as you would have them do to you.

the theme of Jesus as the Son of Man, full of compassion and empathy for all. Luke alone records instances where Jesus wept over Jerusalem and showed deep sympathy towards women, the poor, sinners, the sick, and the dying. This Gospel emphasizes that Jesus' mission was "to seek and to save the lost" (Luke 19:10), culminating in His resurrection. Luke's portrayal reminds us that Jesus' ministry transcends cultural and social boundaries, reaching out to every heart in need.

**Personal Notes:**

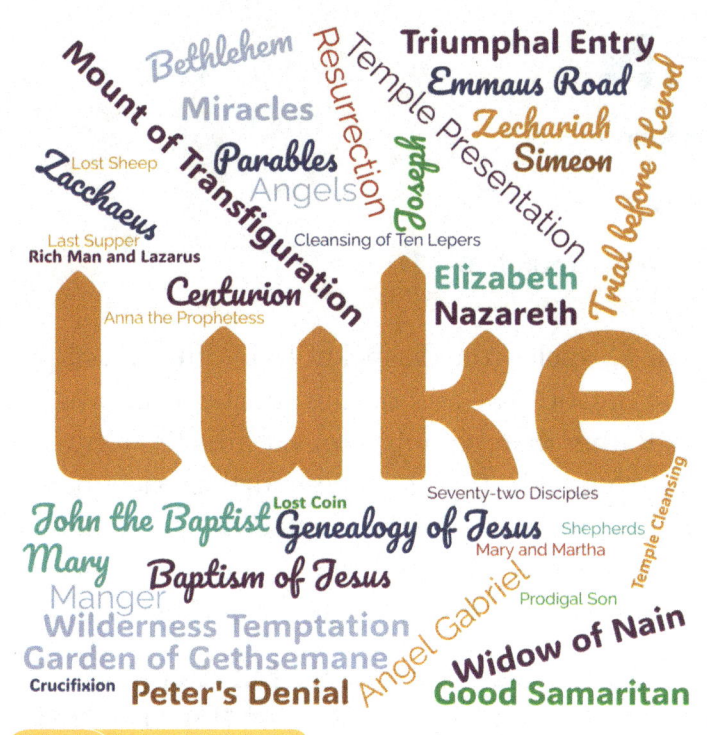

## Reflections on Luke
*Savior for All*

Jesus fulfilled Israel's hopes as their Messiah, ushering in the Kingdom of God. He deliberately guided the events of His life to fulfill His mission, willingly sacrificing Himself for sin through crucifixion. The truths of the gospel are historically affirmed, encompassing Jesus Christ's birth, crucifixion, burial, resurrection, and ascension. Salvation is universally available, extending to every individual. Integral to every believer's spiritual journey is the practice of prayer.

## NOTABLE & POPULAR

**People**

Jesus, Mary, Elizabeth, Zachariah, Peter

**Places**

Bethlehem, Jerusalem, Nazareth, Emmaus

**Events**

Birth of John the Baptist, Birth of Jesus, Crucifixion, Resurrection, Ascension

**Verses**

**Luke 2:7** And she gave birth to her firstborn, a Son. She wrapped Him in swaddling cloths and laid Him in a manger, because there was no room for them in the inn.

**Luke 3:16** John answered all of them: "I baptize you with water, but One more powerful than I will come, the straps of whose sandals I am not worthy to untie. He will baptize you with the Holy Spirit and with fire.

**Luke 18:31-33** Then Jesus took the Twelve aside and said to them, "Look, we are going up to Jerusalem, and everything the prophets have written about the Son of Man will be fulfilled. He will be delivered over to the Gentiles and will be mocked and insulted and spit upon. hey will flog Him and kill Him, and on the third day He will rise again."

# JOHN

**Author:** John

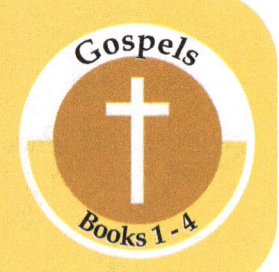

**Time Written:** Likely 85 to 90 A.D.

**Time Covered:** Before Time to Around 30 A.D.

Distinct from Matthew, Mark, and Luke—the Synoptic Gospels—the Gospel of John offers a unique perspective on Jesus Christ, portraying Him as the Son of God. The author, the apostle John, was part of Jesus' inner circle along with Peter and James. Rather than naming himself directly, John humbly refers to himself as "the disciple whom Jesus loved." His Gospel begins further back than the others, highlighting the preincarnate Jesus, known as "the Word," who created the universe (John 1:1-3). This powerful introduction sets the tone for John's emphasis on the divine glory of Christ. John's Gospel is rich with distinctive content and insights into Jesus' nature and mission. It

*A Key Verse:* John 1:14, The Word became flesh and made His dwelling among us. We have seen His glory, the glory of the one and only Son from the Father, full of grace and truth.

begins with the profound declaration that "in Him was life, and that life was the light of men" (John 1:4). John speaks frequently of "life," mentioning it 47 times, and places great emphasis on faith and salvation, noting that "everyone who believes in Him may have eternal life" (John 3:15). John provides in-depth teachings on the role of the Holy Spirit (John 14:26; 16:13-14) and delivers an extensive account of Jesus' instructions and prayer during the Passover meal (John 13-17). His narrative richly documents Jesus' identity as the "Lamb of God" and His mission to save the world through His sacrifice. The central theme of John's Gospel is encapsulated in the verse: "These are

*A Popular Verse:* John 3:16, For God so loved the world that He gave His one and only Son, that everyone who believes in Him shall not perish but have eternal life.

written that you may believe that Jesus is the Christ, the Son of God, and that by believing you may have life in His name" (John 20:31). Throughout the Gospel, John emphasizes the intimate relationship believers can have with God, using the term "Father" 126 times to highlight the divine love accessible to all. His detailed recounting of the Upper Room meal and the events leading up to Jesus' Resurrection serves as the climactic proof of Jesus' divine identity and mission, reinforcing the message of eternal life through faith in Him.

**Personal Notes:**

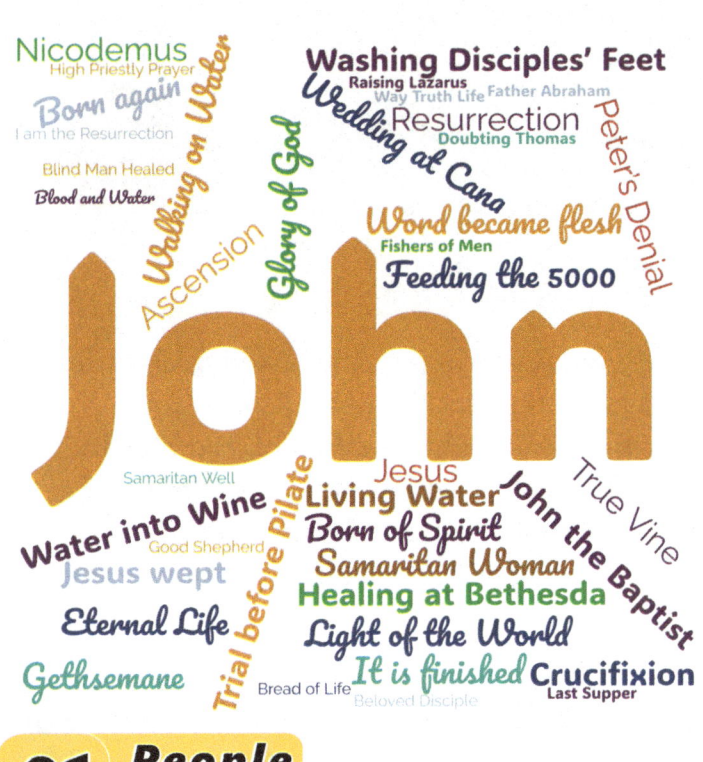

# Reflections on John
*Word Made Flesh*

Jesus is the divine Word who descended from heaven, clothed in human flesh. Although His mission was aimed at the Jews, only a few accepted Him. His many public miracles affirmed His identity as the Messiah, the Son of God. At the heart of Jesus' teachings was the principle that salvation could be found solely through Him.

## NOTABLE & POPULAR

**People**

Jesus, Peter, Lazarus, Mary Magdalene

**Places**

Cana, Capernaum, Samaria, Sea of Galilee

**Events**

Miracles, "I Am" Statements, Farewell Discourse, Crucifixion, Resurrection

**Verses**

**John 11:25** Jesus said to her, "I am the resurrection and the life. Whoever believes in Me will live, even though he dies.

**John 13:35** By this everyone will know that you are My disciples, if you love one another."

**John 14:6** Jesus answered, "I am the way and the truth and the life. No one comes to the Father except through Me.

**John 19:30** When Jesus had received the sour wine, He said, "It is finished." And bowing His head, He yielded up His spirit.

**John 20:29** Jesus said to him, "Because you have seen Me, you have believed; blessed are those who have not seen and yet have believed."

# ACTS

**Author:** Luke

**Time Written:** Likely between 61 and 64 A.D.

**Time Covered:** Around 30 to 62 A.D.

*Acts — New Testament* | *Historic — Book 5*

Jesus' final words before His ascension, "you will be My witnesses in Jerusalem, and in all Judea and Samaria, and to the ends of the earth" (Acts 1:8), set the stage for the remarkable events recorded in the Book of Acts. Filled with the Holy Spirit, the early Christians embraced this divine mandate, spreading the message of the risen Savior far and wide. As the second installment of a two-part work by Luke, the Book of Acts originally may not have had a distinct title but is designated in Greek manuscripts as Praxeis, or "Acts," referring to the notable deeds of prominent individuals. Though the apostles are often referenced collectively, the book primarily focuses on the

**A Key Verse:** Acts 2:38, Peter replied, "Repent and be baptized, every one of you, in the name of Jesus Christ for the forgiveness of your sins, and you will receive the gift of the Holy Spirit.

ministries of Peter (Acts 1-12) and Paul (Acts 13-28). The Book of Acts details the early church's first three decades after Jesus' resurrection, chronicling pivotal moments from Jerusalem to Rome. Peter emerges as a key leader in Jerusalem, guiding the fledgling church, while Paul extends Christianity's reach to the Gentiles beyond Israel. The book not only documents the astonishing achievements and rapid growth of the early Christian movement but also honestly addresses its struggles and conflicts (e.g., Acts 5:1-11; 11:1-2; 15:1-5,15:36-40). This balanced account provides a realistic portrayal of the early church's journey, capturing its triumphs as well as its trials. The

**A Popular Verse:** Acts 1:8, But you will receive power when the Holy Spirit comes upon you, and you will be My witnesses in Jerusalem, and in all Judea and Samaria, and to the ends of the earth."

central theme of Acts is the apostles' steadfast preaching of the resurrected Christ and the vital role of the Holy Spirit. The text vividly portrays how the Holy Spirit empowered, guided, protected, and encouraged early believers to serve as bold witnesses for Jesus. This divine support enabled them to overcome persecution, cultural barriers, and internal challenges, ensuring that the message of salvation reached "the ends of the earth" as Jesus told them they would, just before He ascended to heaven. The Book of Acts stands as a testament to the transformative power of the Holy Spirit and the unwavering faith of those first Christians.

**Personal Notes:**

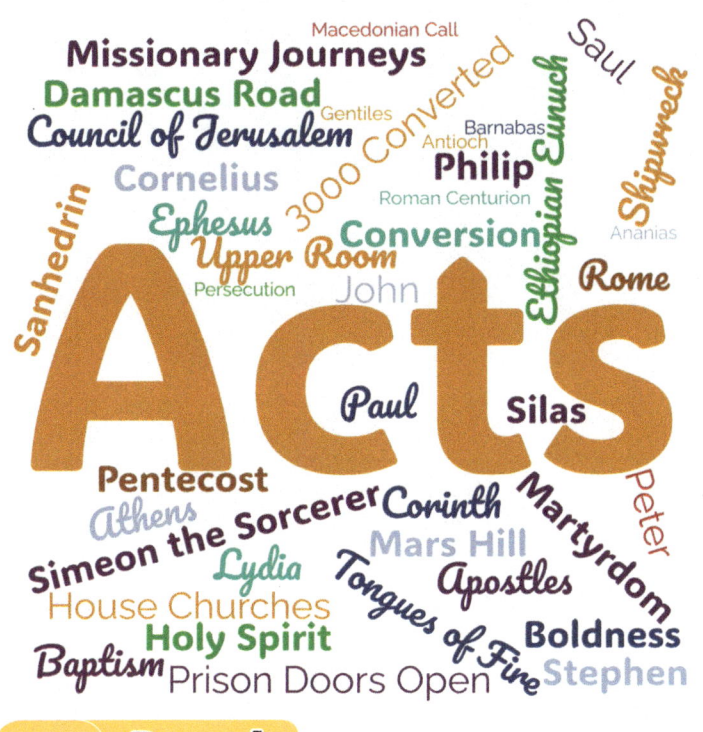

## Reflections on Acts
*Church's Birth*

Christ's witnesses are empowered by the Holy Spirit, enabling them to spread His message to the ends of the earth. A shared experience among Christ's witnesses is the endurance of persecution. They plant churches that carry forward Christ's mission, ensuring the ongoing proclamation of His gospel.

## NOTABLE & POPULAR

**People**

Peter, Paul, Stephen, Barnabas, Philip

**Places**

Jerusalem, Ephesus, Corinth, Rome

**Events**

Pentecost, Spread of the Gospel, Paul's Missionary Journeys, Jerusalem Council

**Verses**

**Acts 4:12** Salvation exists in no one else, for there is no other name under heaven given to men by which we must be saved."

**Acts 4:19-20** But Peter and John replied, "Judge for yourselves whether it is right in God's sight to listen to you rather than God. For we cannot stop speaking about what we have seen and heard."

**Acts 9:3-6** As Saul drew near to Damascus on his journey, suddenly a light from heaven flashed around him. He fell to the ground and heard a voice say to him, "Saul, Saul, why do you persecute Me?" "Who are You, Lord?" Saul asked. "I am Jesus, whom you are persecuting," He replied. "Now get up and go into the city, and you will be told what you must do."

# PAULINE EPISTLES

Following the gospels and the book of Acts, we encounter the epistles written by the apostle Paul. These letters primarily delve into doctrinal teachings essential for the early Christian communities and for us today. Starting with the book of Romans, Paul provides a comprehensive and profound discussion on salvation, underlining the grace and righteousness that come through faith in Jesus Christ. His writings span across various aspects of the Christian life, offering guidance on how believers should live in accordance with God's will.

Paul's epistles also address the structure and functioning of the church. He outlines roles within the church, emphasizes unity and love among believers, and offers practical advice on handling everyday challenges within the Christian community. Furthermore, Paul writes extensively about the second coming of Christ and the eventual rise of the Antichrist, preparing believers for the future and encouraging them to stay steadfast in their faith. His letters serve as foundational texts for understanding the Christian faith and building a strong, doctrinally sound church.

In addition to instruction and encouragement, Paul issues warnings about the dangers posed by false teachers and their deceptive doctrines. Through his letters, he equips believers with solid, biblical truths to counteract these errors and maintain their fidelity to the gospel. By rooting Christians in sound doctrine, Paul ensures that the early church, and by extension today's church, remains anchored in the truth, growing in spiritual maturity, and resilient against false teachings. His epistles continue to offer timeless wisdom and encouragement, helping believers to navigate their faith journey with confidence and hope.

**Personal Notes:**

# ROMANS

**Author:** Paul

**Time Written:** Likely between 57 and 58 A.D.

**Time Covered:** Around 57 A.D.

Romans — New Testament

Pauline Epistles — Books 6 - 18

The Epistle to the Romans, authored by the apostle Paul, is a cornerstone in the New Testament and is positioned first among his thirteen epistles or 'formal letters.' Unlike the four Gospels, which recount the words and deeds of Jesus Christ, Romans delves into the significance of Christ's sacrificial death. Paul provides a methodical account of biblical doctrine, highlighting pivotal topics like salvation and faith, making it a crucial text for understanding core Christian beliefs. Beyond theology (or religious theory and belief), Romans offers practical advice on living a life of joyful obedience to God. It teaches that the Good News of Jesus Christ is more than just facts to be

**A Key Verse:** Romans 1:16, I am not ashamed of the gospel, because it is the power of God for salvation to everyone who believes, first to the Jew, then to the Greek.

believed—it is an abundant life to be lived, reflecting the righteousness bestowed upon those justified by God's grace through Jesus Christ. Reformers like Martin Luther found profound inspiration in this epistle; for instance, "The righteous will live by faith" (Rom. 1:17) led Luther to understand that salvation comes not through works or rituals, but through faith in God's unearned grace. Good works are thus seen not as a path to salvation, but as a grateful response to it. Paul opens his letter by emphasizing the importance of love and humility in obeying the Lord. He reminds readers that eternal life and the grace to face every circumstance come through Jesus

**A Popular Verse:** Romans 8:28, And we know that God works all things together for the good of those who love Him, who are called according to His purpose.

Christ, who liberates believers from the power of sin. Romans underscores the necessity of recognizing our need for a Savior to truly appreciate God's gracious gift. Titled "To the Romans," the epistle's central message is that people everywhere can enjoy God's gift of eternal salvation through faith in Jesus Christ, who empowers them with the desire and strength to obey the Lord.

**Personal Notes:**

# Romans

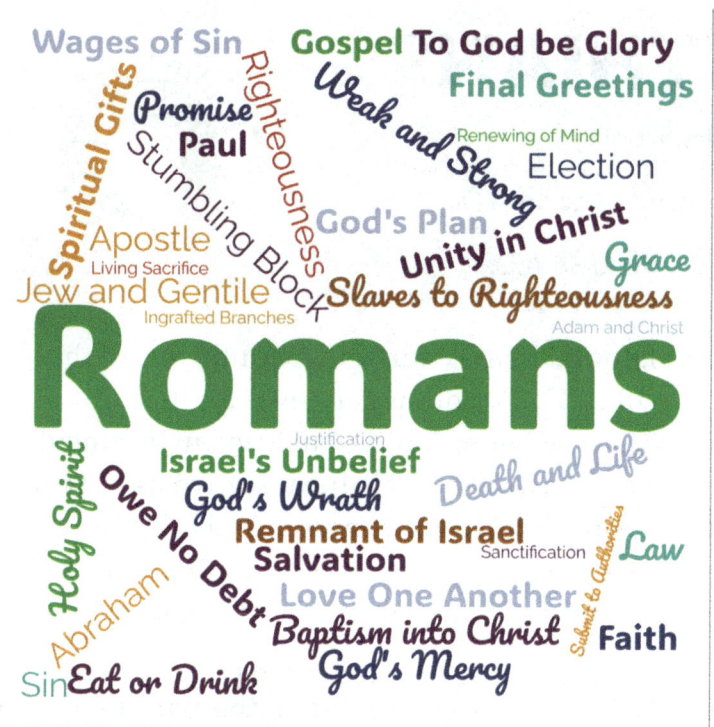

## Reflections on Romans
*Justification by Faith*

Jews and Gentiles alike are sinners under God's judgment. Their justification comes through faith alone, apart from works. The path to glorification involves sanctification, which is sustained by dependence on the Holy Spirit. Throughout history, Jews and Gentiles have held interconnected roles. It is essential for both Jewish and Gentile Christians to apply the gospel to the practical aspects of daily life.

## Notable & Popular

**People**

Paul, Phoebe, Priscilla, Aquila, Tertius

**Places**

Rome, Jerusalem (referenced)

**Events**

Paul's Teachings on Faith, Justification, Salvation, Christian Living

**Verses**

**Romans 8:9** You, however, are controlled not by the flesh, but by the Spirit, if the Spirit of God lives in you. And if anyone does not have the Spirit of Christ, he does not belong to Christ.

**Romans 10:9** that if you confess with your mouth, "Jesus is Lord," and believe in your heart that God raised Him from the dead, you will be saved.

**Romans 12:1** Therefore I urge you, brothers, on account of God's mercy, to offer your bodies as living sacrifices, holy and pleasing to God, which is your spiritual service of worship.

**Romans 12:19** Do not avenge yourselves, beloved, but leave room for God's wrath. For it is written: "Vengeance is Mine; I will repay, says the Lord."

# 1 CORINTHIANS

**Author:** Paul

**Time Written:** Around 55 to 56 A.D.

**Time Covered:** Around 54 A.D.

The Apostle Paul, a passionate advocate of the Gospel, founded the church in Corinth, one of the most influential cities in Greece during his time (Acts 18:1-17). Corinth was known for its commerce, but also for its degraded culture and idolatrous religion. Amidst such an environment, Paul established a Christian community and later addressed two letters to them, known as First and Second Corinthians. First Corinthians, in particular, reveals Paul's deep concern for the young church, which was struggling to separate itself from the prevailing pagan society. In this letter, Paul tackles a variety of pressing issues within the Corinthian church. These included factions and

**A Key Verse:** 1 Corinthians 15:3-4, For what I received I passed on to you as of first importance: that Christ died for our sins according to the Scriptures, that He was buried, that He was raised on the third day according to the Scriptures,

divisions, lawsuits among believers, immorality, and the misuse of the Lord's Supper and spiritual gifts. He writes with both authority and compassion, offering counsel on these matters, often referencing specific inquiries made by the Corinthian believers themselves (1 Cor. 1:11; 7:1; 8:1; 12:1; 16:1). Paul also mentions earlier attempts to guide the church, including a previously written, now lost letter warning against immorality (5:9-10). His intention was not only to correct but to nurture the church towards spiritual maturity. The central message of First Corinthians revolves around God's desire for believers to live in a way that honors Christ, despite the corrupt culture

**A Popular Verse:** 1 Corinthians 13:4-5, Love is patient, love is kind. It does not envy, it does not boast, it is not proud. It is not rude, it is not self-seeking, it is not easily angered, it keeps no account of wrongs.

surrounding them. Paul's instructions aimed to help the Corinthian church establish a more solid, spiritual foundation. He also expressed his plans to visit them personally to address any unresolved issues (4:19, 21; 16:5). The letter, historically titled "Pros Korinthious A," focuses on teaching the early Christians how to align their lives with the will of God, serving as a timeless guide for believers facing the challenges of a secular world.

**Personal Notes:**

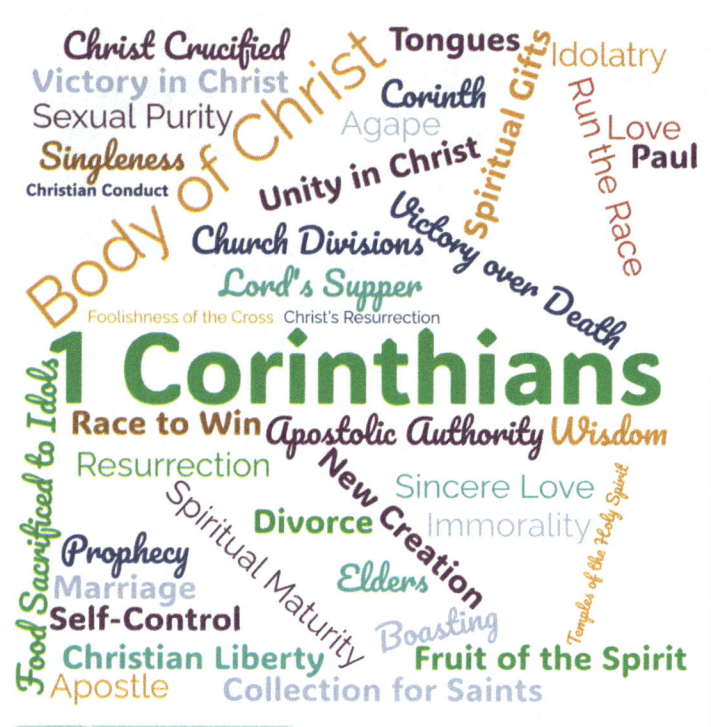

# Reflections on 1 Corinthians
## *Church Problems*

The Church must be built on the pillar of unity, not division. Christians should seek wisdom from God as their model, rather than adhering to worldly standards. The establishment and execution of proper church governance and discipline help maintain the Church's peace and purity. The exercise of Christian liberty should be considerate of those with weaker faith. In worship and the use of spiritual gifts, the emphasis should be to honor God and respect fellow believers. The future bodily resurrection of believers is a core tenet of the Gospel.

## NOTABLE & POPULAR

**People**

Paul, Chloe, Apollos, Peter

**Places**

Corinth, Ephesus (where likely written)

**Events**

Addressing Divisions, Moral Issues, Resurrection Doctrine, Spiritual Gifts

**Verses**

**1 Corinthians 3:3** for you are still worldly. For since there is jealousy and dissension among you, are you not worldly? Are you not walking in the way of man?

**1 Corinthians 6:19-20** Do you not know that your body is a temple of the Holy Spirit who is in you, whom you have received from God? You are not your own; you were bought at a price. Therefore glorify God with your body.

**1 Corinthians 10:31** So whether you eat or drink or whatever you do, do it all to the glory of God.

**1 Corinthians 12:7** Now to each one the manifestation of the Spirit is given for the common good.

# 2 CORINTHIANS

**Author:** Paul

**Time Written:** Likely between 55 and 57 A.D.

**Time Covered:** Around 55 to 57 A.D.

In the wake of Paul's first letter to the Corinthians, false teachers infiltrated the church, sowing discord and urging believers to dismiss Paul's teachings. These detractors painted Paul as out of touch, prideful, and lacking the qualities worthy of an apostle. By the time Paul penned 2 Corinthians, the situation had evolved, with the church beginning to recognize their errors and the creeping influence of sin. Paul had sent Titus to Corinth to address these issues and uplift the congregation's faith. Titus returned with encouraging news, prompting Paul to write this heartfelt letter expressing thanksgiving for the repentant majority and urging any lingering rebellious

**A Key Verse:** 2 Corinthians 5:7, For we walk by faith, not by sight.

members to submit to his apostolic authority. Second Corinthians uniquely emphasizes Paul's personal defense of his apostleship and his deep emotional connection with the Corinthian church. The letter also contains the New Testament's longest discussion on the grace of giving, spanning chapters 8 and 9. Paul explains that generosity mirrors Christ's sacrifice, reminding us that Jesus, though rich, became poor for our sake. Paul underscores the principle of cheerful giving, affirming that those who sow generously will also reap generously. His counsel not only encourages material generosity but also reflects the transformative power of a generous spirit. At its core, 2 Corinthians

**A Popular Verse:** 2 Corinthians 5:17, Therefore if anyone is in Christ, he is a new creation. The old has passed away. Behold, the new has come!

is a poignant defense of Paul's ministry and a testament to the power of humble, Christ-centered leadership amidst adversity. Paul openly shares his sufferings for Christ, recounts his mystical experience of visiting "the third heaven," and speaks candidly about his "thorn in the flesh," through which he learned the paradox of strength in weakness. This epistle's central theme is the vindication of Paul's apostolic ministry, reassuring believers of the divine authority behind his teachings and encouraging unwavering faith in the truth of the gospel.

**Personal Notes:**

# Reflections on 2 Corinthians
*Apostolic Defense*

In times of suffering, Christians should find comfort and encouragement in God's nurturing care. God's strength is remarkably revealed through human weakness. The magnificent fulfillment of the Old Covenant's promises is achieved through the New Covenant in Christ. Christians share a collective duty to help meet each other's material needs.

## NOTABLE & POPULAR

**People**

Paul, Titus

**Places**

Corinth, Macedonia (where written)

**Events**

Defense of Paul's Apostleship, Collection for the Saints, Christian Ministry

**Verses**

**2 Corinthians 3:5** Not that we are competent in ourselves to claim that anything comes from us, but our competence comes from God.

**2 Corinthians 3:18** And we, who with unveiled faces all reflect the glory of the Lord, are being transformed into His image with intensifying glory, which comes from the Lord, who is the Spirit.

**2 Corinthians 5:21** God made Him who knew no sin to be sin on our behalf, so that in Him we might become the righteousness of God.

**2 Corinthians 10:5** We tear down arguments and every presumption set up against the knowledge of God; and we take captive every thought to make it obedient to Christ.

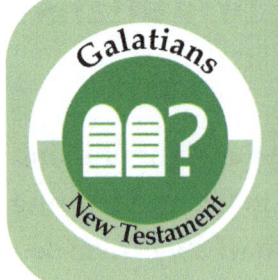

# GALATIANS

**Author:** Paul

**Time Written:** Either 48 to 49 or 53 to 54 A.D.

**Time Covered:** Uncertain - between 48 and 54 A.D.

The Apostle Paul had been a member of the Pharisees, a Jewish 'legalistic' sect who'd believed in a strict interpretation of all laws but also in ungodly and hypocritical traditions that had been passed down by their leaders. Then Paul miraculously encountered Jesus, on the road to Damascus and converted to Christianity. Shortly after founding several churches in the region of Galatia, Paul wrote this letter to address a pressing controversy. Jewish Christians were insisting that Gentile (non-Jewish) believers must follow traditional Jewish laws and customs to achieve salvation. This ongoing conflict between grace and legalistic works mirrored debates occurring in Jerusalem and

*A Key Verse:* Galatians 2:20, I have been crucified with Christ, and I no longer live, but Christ lives in me. The life I live in the body, I live by faith in the Son of God, who loved me and gave Himself up for me.

Syrian Antioch, as described in Acts 15. Paul's letter to the Galatians stands out for its fervent defense of the doctrine of justification by faith in Jesus Christ. He emphasizes that believers are not justified by the works of the law but by faith alone. Paul boldly asserts his apostolic authority, declaring that his message came directly from God. He stresses that blessings come from the Lord through obedience and faith rather than through ritualistic adherence. While the law exposes humanity's guilt, Paul highlights that Jesus' grace liberates us, allowing believers to experience true freedom in Christ. However, this freedom is not a license to sin, but an invitation to walk in the

*A Popular Verse:* Galatians 5:22-23, But the fruit of the Spirit is love, joy, peace, patience, kindness, goodness, faithfulness, gentleness, and self-control. Against such things there is no law.

Spirit and bear righteous fruit. At its heart, the message of Galatians underscores the futility of trying to earn God's favor through human efforts. Paul urges the Galatian Christians to remember the joy and freedom they first experienced through faith, not through self-reliant works. He calls them to live empowered by the Holy Spirit, capable of overcoming fleshly desires and honoring God with their lives. Addressed explicitly "to the churches of Galatia," this epistle serves as a potent reminder that salvation is a gift from God, accessible through faith in Jesus Christ alone. The central theme reverberates with the reassurance that true righteousness and joy come from following Jesus and relying on the Holy Spirit's guidance.

**Personal Notes:**

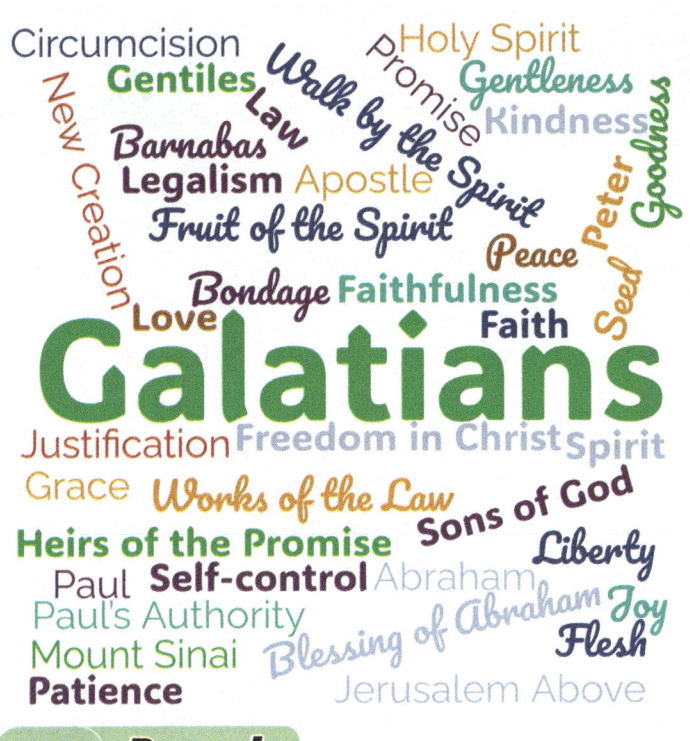

# Reflections on Galatians
*Freedom in Christ*

Justification before God is achieved solely through faith. Sanctification in daily life is powered by faith through the Holy Spirit. Paul's message, which underscores salvation by faith apart from works, is reliable. The concept of salvation by faith is a consistent thread throughout all Scriptures. Legalism diverts us from Christ and leads to futility and judgment. Freedom from legalism means the liberty to live for Christ, driven by the Spirit. Eternal salvation is granted exclusively to those who embed their faith and lives in the true Gospel.

## NOTABLE & POPULAR

**People**

Paul, Peter, James (the Lord's brother)

**Places**

Galatia, Jerusalem (referenced)

**Events**

Defense of the Gospel, Faith and Law, Fruits of the Spirit

**Verses**

**Galatians 2:16** know that a man is not justified by works of the law, but by faith in Jesus Christ. So we, too, have believed in Christ Jesus, that we may be justified by faith in Christ and not by works of the law, because by works of the law no one will be justified.

**Galatians 3:11** Now it is clear that no one is justified before God by the law, because, "The righteous will live by faith."

**Galatians 4:5-6** to redeem those under the law, that we might receive our adoption as sons. And because you are sons, God sent the Spirit of His Son into our hearts, crying out, "Abba, Father!"

**Galatians 6:7** Do not be deceived: God is not to be mocked. Whatever a man sows, he will reap in return.

117

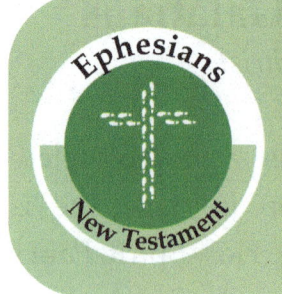

# EPHESIANS

**Author:** Paul

**Time Written:** Likely between 60 and 63 A.D.

**Time Covered:** Around 60 to 62 A.D.

Ephesians, believed to be authored by the Apostle Paul, speaks to a community of believers who, though abundant in spiritual wealth through Jesus Christ, lived as if in poverty. Paul, with his deep pastoral heart, wrote this letter to illuminate their true riches in Christ. He sought to pull them out of ignorance regarding their profound standing as God's children, sealed with the Holy Spirit. This epistle, or letter, emphasizes that Christians are endowed with unparalleled spiritual blessings, yet these can only be fully realized through understanding and faith. Within the letter, we find unique and intriguing content. Though traditionally titled "To the Ephesians," there is scholarly debate

**A Key Verse:** Ephesians 4:1-2, As a prisoner in the Lord, then, I urge you to walk in a manner worthy of the calling you have received: with all humility and gentleness, with patience, bearing with one another in love,

about its intended recipients due to variations in ancient manuscripts. Some suggest it was meant as a circular letter to several churches in Asia, given its general lack of addressing specific local issues. Regardless of the audience, whether the Ephesians alone or broader congregations, the letter's timeless and universal message has provided spiritual nourishment and guidance across generations. The core message of Ephesians centers on the immense spiritual blessings available in Christ and the unity of the church. Through vivid imagery and profound theological - or religious scholarly - insights, Paul reveals the mystery of God's plan—to bring unity to all things in heaven

**A Popular Verse:** Ephesians 2:8-9, For it is by grace you have been saved through faith, and this not from yourselves; it is the gift of God, not by works, so that no one can boast.

and on earth under Christ. He calls believers to live in a manner worthy of their calling, fostering unity and building one another up in love. This epistle not only underscores their spiritual inheritance but also encourages a life of faith and communal harmony, reflecting God's grand design for His church.

**Personal Notes:**

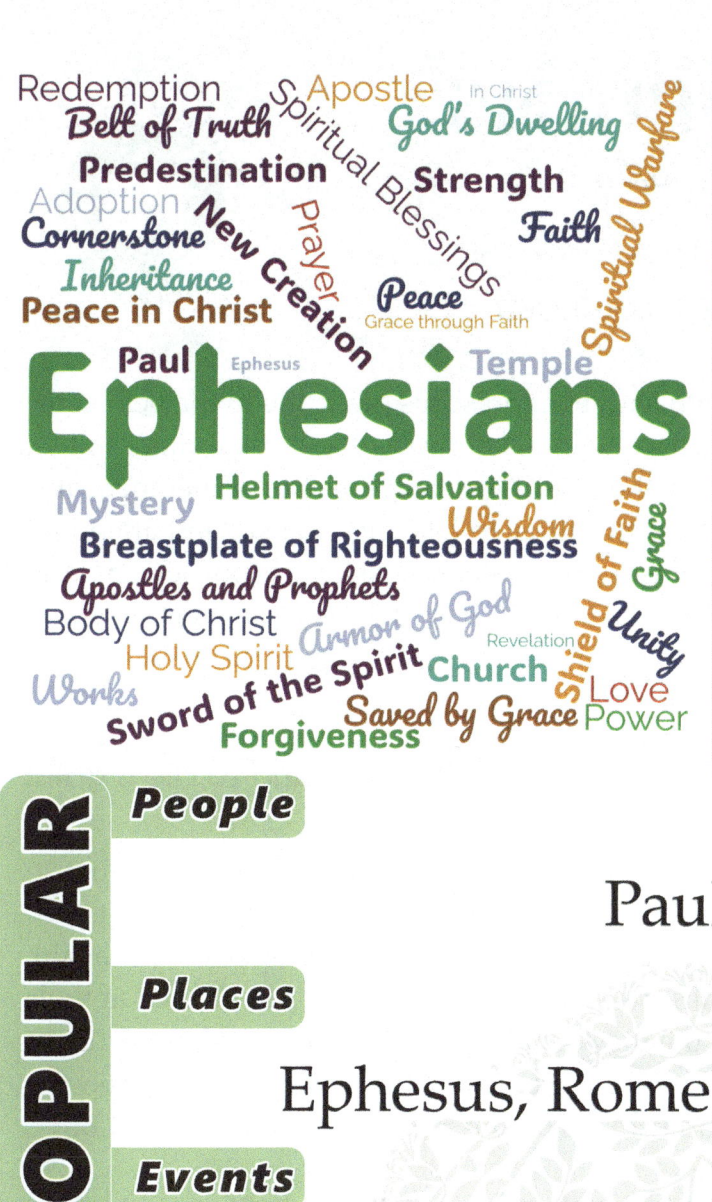

# Reflections on Ephesians
*Unity in Christ*

In union with Christ, the Church has been endowed with extraordinary blessings. Through Christ, the Church has transitioned from death to life. Promised to extend globally, the Church will unite Jews and Gentiles in Christ. Pursuing unity in Christ is an essential mission for the Church. The Church's conduct should reflect the ways of Christ, avoiding a return to worldly sinful behaviors. In Christ, the Church must find the strength required for spiritual warfare.

## Notable & Popular

**People**

Paul, Tychicus

**Places**

Ephesus, Rome (where likely written)

**Events**

Unity in Christ, Christian Conduct, Armor of God

**Verses**

**Ephesians 1:3** Blessed be the God and Father of our Lord Jesus Christ, who has blessed us in Christ with every spiritual blessing in the heavenly realms.

**Ephesians 4:4-6** There is one body and one Spirit, just as you were called to one hope when you were called; one Lord, one faith, one baptism; one God and Father of all, who is over all and through all and in all.

**Ephesians 5:21** Submit to one another out of reverence for Christ.

**Ephesians 6:10-11** Finally, be strong in the Lord and in His mighty power. Put on the full armor of God, so that you can make your stand against the devil's schemes.

# PHILIPPIANS

**Author:** Paul

**Time Written:** Likely around 62 A.D.

**Time Covered:** Around 62 A.D.

*Pauline Epistles, Books 6 - 18*

Philippians is a heartfelt letter penned by the apostle Paul to express his gratitude to the believers in the city of Philippi for their support during a difficult time in his ministry. Paul was writing to them from a Roman prison, for having proclaimed Jesus as the risen Lord, and the church members at Philippi had sent a fellow member, a man named Epaphroditus, to take gifts to Paul and attend to his needs . Paul had founded the church in Philippi during his second missionary journey, making it the first church established in Macedonia. This letter is filled with Paul's personal affection and warmth, reflecting his deep relationship with the Philippian believers. In Philippians, Paul

**A Key Verse:** Philippians 1:21, For to me, to live is Christ, and to die is gain.

highlights unique content by sharing his personal experiences and insights. He emphasizes that true joy and unity are found only in Christ, regardless of circumstances. Paul's imprisonment becomes a testament to this, as he conveys how his chains have furthered the gospel, even reaching the palace guard. By drawing on his own trials, Paul encourages the Philippians to be bold in their faith, demonstrating that God can transform even the most challenging situations into opportunities for joy and growth. The central message of Philippians revolves around the themes of unity, joy, and steadfast faith. Paul urges the believers to stand firm, be of one mind, and rejoice in the Lord

**A Popular Verse:** Philippians 4:13, I can do all things through Christ who gives me strength.

always. He teaches that through prayer, supplication, and thanksgiving, believers can experience the peace of God, which surpasses all understanding. This epistle serves as a comforting reminder that the Christian life is meant to be a joyful journey, enriched by the unity and community found in Christ.

**Personal Notes:**

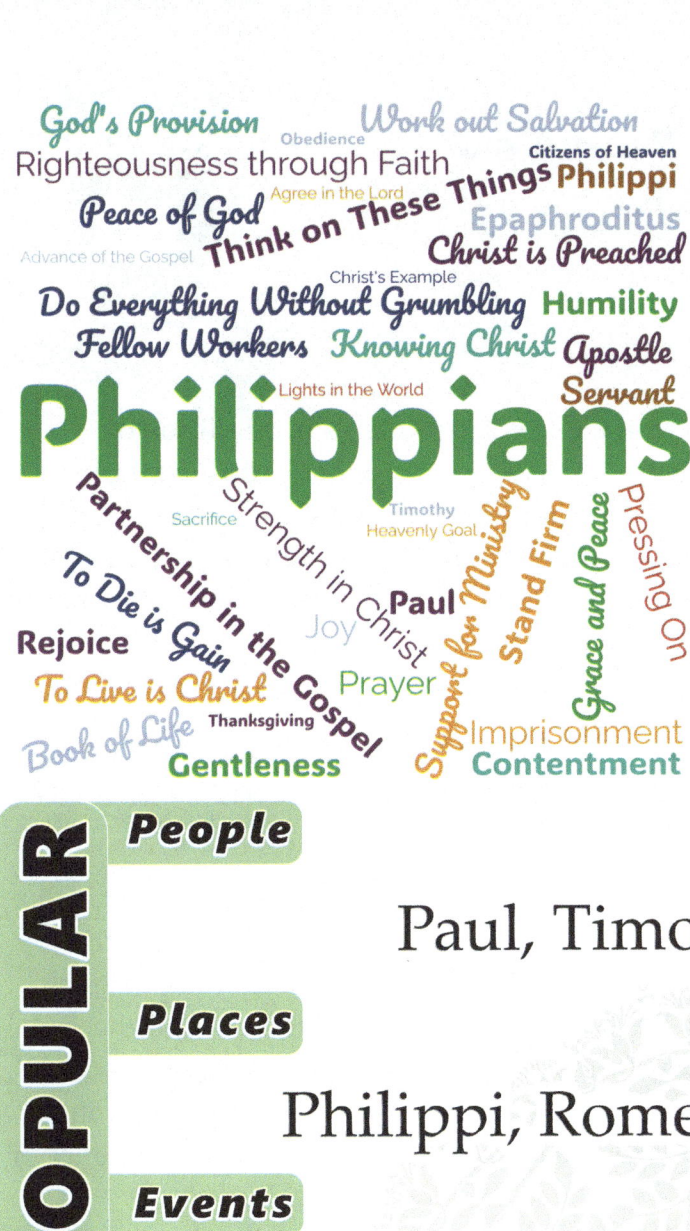

# Reflections on Philippians
*Joy in Christ*

The gospel of Christ endures, undeterred by the trials of persecution. Suffering for Christ, regarded as a privilege, paves the path to glory for believers. A genuine manifestation of the Gospel in believers' lives is demonstrated through serving one another, following Christ's example. Believers are encouraged to resolutely uphold the truth while avoiding extremes like legalism or - on the other hand - believing that Christians are not bound by God's moral laws, at all. Supporting others in ministry is a crucial aspect of Christian practice.

## NOTABLE & POPULAR

**People**

Paul, Timothy, Epaphroditus

**Places**

Philippi, Rome (where likely written)

**Events**

Joy in Suffering, Unity, Humility, Exhortation

**Verses**

**Philippians 1:6** being confident of this, that He who began a good work in you will carry it on to completion until the day of Christ Jesus.

**Philippians 3:7** But whatever was gain to me I count as loss for the sake of Christ.

**Philippians 4:4** Rejoice in the Lord always. I will say it again: Rejoice!

**Philippians 4:6-7** Be anxious for nothing, but in everything, by prayer and petition, with thanksgiving, present your requests to God. And the peace of God, which surpasses all understanding, will guard your hearts and your minds in Christ Jesus.

# COLOSSIANS

**Author:** Paul

**Time Written:** Likely around 62 A.D.

**Time Covered:** Around 62 A.D.

Written by Paul during his imprisonment, the letter to the Colossians follows his tradition of shepherding fledgling congregations through written guidance. Paul, an apostle chosen by Christ, penned this letter to address some troubling developments in the young church at Colossae. He sought to correct errors and remind the believers of their foundational truths. The church was likely established by Epaphras, a devoted follower whom Paul had mentored, and Paul wrote with a heart full of pastoral care and concern. In this epistle, Paul emphasizes the supremacy and sufficiency of Jesus Christ. Through vivid descriptions and profound declarations, he portrays Jesus as the image

**A Key Verse:** Colossians 1:27, To them God has chosen to make known among the Gentiles the glorious riches of this mystery, which is Christ in you, the hope of glory.

of the invisible God and the Creator and Sustainer of everything, visible and invisible. Christ is presented as the eternal Creator, the one who holds all things together, the first to rise from the dead in an everlasting sense, and the sole Savior of humanity. Paul also underlines Jesus' roles as the Lord of life, victorious over all spiritual powers, the benevolent Master of heaven, and the rewarding Lord for all faithful believers. Each of these facets serves to highlight that Christ is unparalleled and integral to the Christian faith. The primary theme of Colossians revolves around the centrality and preeminence of Jesus Christ. Paul wrote to counteract the destructive influence of

**A Popular Verse:** Colossians 3:23, Whatever you do, work at it with your whole being, for the Lord and not for men,

syncretism, where the Colossian believers had started mixing pagan philosophies with Christian doctrine. Firmly reminding them that their faith and lives must be anchored solely in Christ, Paul calls for an authentic and undivided allegiance to Jesus. He encourages believers to live rooted, alive, hidden, and complete in Christ, with His peace and love guiding their hearts. This focused dedication to Jesus equips believers to navigate challenges and remain faithful, making Him foremost in all aspects of their lives.

**Personal Notes:**

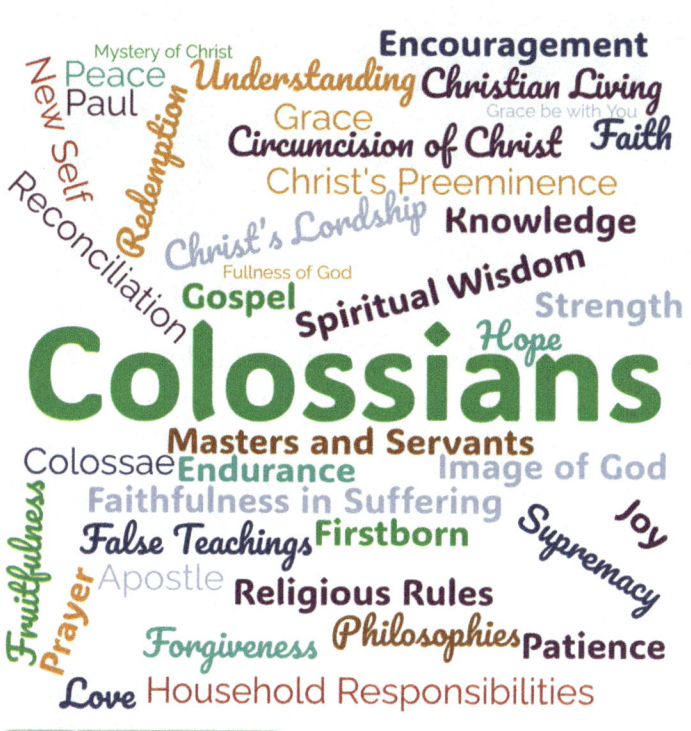

# Reflections on Colossians
*Christ's Supremacy*

Christ is unparalleled in His supremacy over all creation and the Church. Believers must remain vigilant against the confusion caused by false belief standards that blend true faith with counterfeit religions or philosophies. Christ embodies perfect sufficiency, bringing wholeness and renewal to believers' lives. Christians are called to live in reliance on Christ and His power, rather than any other source of strength.

## NOTABLE & POPULAR

**People**

Paul, Timothy, Epaphras

**Places**

Colossae, Rome (where likely written)

**Events**

Supremacy of Christ, Christian Living

**Verses**

**Colossians 1:15-16** The Son is the image of the invisible God, the firstborn over all creation. For in Him all things were created, things in heaven and on earth, visible and invisible, whether thrones or dominions or rulers or authorities. All things were created through Him and for Him.

**Colossians 2:8** See to it that no one takes you captive through philosophy and empty deception, which are based on human tradition and the spiritual forces of the world rather than on Christ.

**Colossians 3:12-13** Therefore, as the elect of God, holy and beloved, clothe yourselves with hearts of compassion, kindness, humility, gentleness, and patience. Bear with one another and forgive any complaint you may have against someone else. Forgive as the Lord forgave you.

# 1 THESSALONIANS

**Author:** Paul

**Time Written:** Likely between 51 to 52 A.D.

**Time Covered:** Around 51 A.D.

Paul cherished his time with the Thessalonian believers, holding dear the faith, hope, love, and perseverance they exhibited amid severe persecution. As a spiritual parent to the fledgling church, Paul's heart was warmed by their steadfastness. He founded the Thessalonian church during his second missionary journey, despite significant opposition from the Jews (Acts 17:1-9). Although his stay was brief, ranging from a few weeks to a few months, his concern for their well-being continued as he moved to Athens. Fearful that the young congregation might falter under continued antagonism, he sent Timothy to support them. Timothy's report, encouraging yet mixed with some

**A Key Verse:** 1 Thessalonians 4:16, For the Lord Himself will descend from heaven with a loud command, with the voice of an archangel, and with the trumpet of God, and the dead in Christ will be the first to rise.

concerns, prompted Paul to write this compassionate letter. The content of Paul's letter to the Thessalonian church is both heartfelt and instructive. He praised them for their burgeoning faith and encouraged them to grow in their love for one another. Paul urged them to rejoice, pray, and give thanks in all circumstances, fortifying their hearts against the trials they faced. A distinctive feature of this letter is that Paul concludes every chapter with a reminder of the Lord's imminent return, offering both hope and a call to persistent faith. These unique touches highlight Paul's tender relationship with this community and his profound commitment to their spiritual growth.

**A Popular Verse:** 1 Thessalonians 5:16-18, Rejoice at all times. Pray without ceasing. Give thanks in every circumstance, for this is God's will for you in Christ Jesus.

Central to this letter is Paul's emphasis on the Second Coming of Christ. He weaves this vital doctrine throughout, demonstrating its importance even to a young church. By consistently reminding the Thessalonians of Jesus' return, Paul lays a foundational teaching meant to sustain and mature their Christian faith. This focus on Christ's advent is a reminder that the anticipation of Jesus' return should encourage believers, comforting them and propelling them to live faithfully. Paul's message is clear: the certainty of Christ's return is a source of hope and should be a key aspect of every believer's life.

**Personal Notes:**

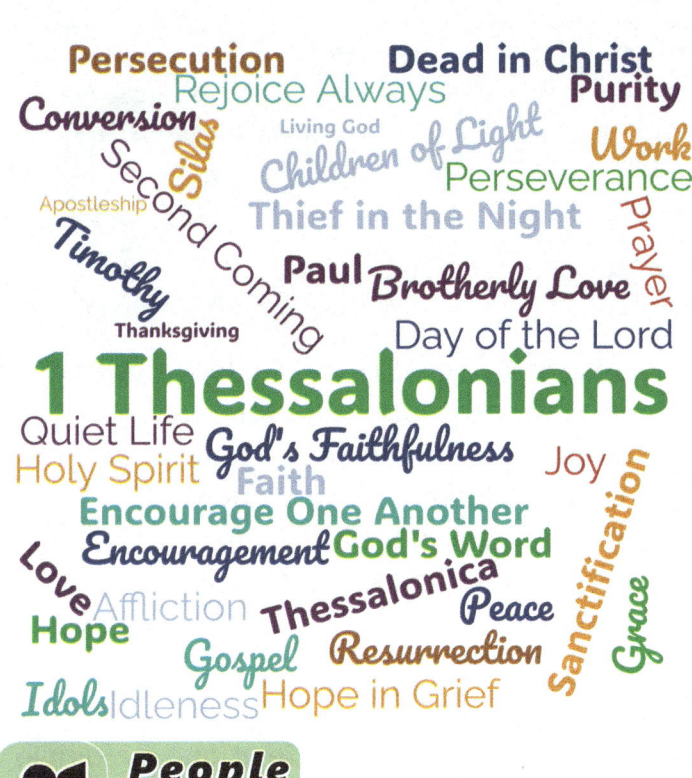

## Reflections on 1 Thessalonians
*Second Coming*

Gratitude should be offered to God for the unwavering faithfulness of His people. Believers deserve commendation for their steadfast faith. It is vital for believers to lead lives that are pleasing to God. At Christ's return, all believers who have died will be resurrected. Maintaining readiness for Christ's return should be a constant mindset for believers.

## NOTABLE & POPULAR

**People**

Paul, Silas, Timothy

**Places**

Thessalonica, Corinth (where written)

**Events**

Encouragement in Persecution, Explaining the Second Coming

**Verses**

**1 Thessalonians 3:5** For this reason, when I could bear it no longer, I sent to find out about your faith, for fear that the tempter had somehow tempted you and caused our labor to be in vain.

**1 Thessalonians 3:7** For this reason, brothers, in all our distress and persecution, we have been reassured about you, because of your faith.

**1 Thessalonians 4:14-15** For since we believe that Jesus died and rose again, we also believe that God will bring with Jesus those who have fallen asleep in Him. By the word of the Lord, we declare to you that we who are alive and remain until the coming of the Lord will by no means precede those who have fallen asleep.

# 2 THESSALONIANS

**Author:** Paul

**Time Written:** Likely around 52 A.D.

**Time Covered:** Around 52 A.D.

Paul's second letter to the Thessalonians was written in response to confusion and doctrinal errors that crept into the church after his first letter. Paul, deeply concerned for the spiritual well-being of the Thessalonian believers, took it upon himself to address these issues head-on. He starts by acknowledging and encouraging their commitment and faith amid severe persecution. Paul reassures them that the trials they are enduring are not in vain but will lead to a future glory that far outweighs their present suffering. A significant portion of Paul's letter is dedicated to correcting a critical misunderstanding about the Second Coming of Jesus Christ. False teachers had spread the

**A Key Verse:** 2 Thessalonians 2:13, But we should always thank God for you, brothers who are loved by the Lord, because God has chosen you from the beginning to be saved by the sanctification of the Spirit and by faith in the truth.

rumor that Christ had already returned, causing anguish among the Thessalonians who feared they had been left behind. Paul counteracts this by assuring them that Jesus had not yet come and explaining the sequence of events that would occur before His return. He specifically notes that there will first be a falling away, where a substantial number of believers will abandon their faith. Paul outlines three key occurrences that would precede the return of Christ: the apostasy, or defection, of the church, the revelation of the "man of sin" or the Antichrist, and the removal of "what is now restraining him" or 'holding back' the Antichrist. This 'restrainer' is likely the Holy

**A Popular Verse:** 2 Thessalonians 3:3, But the Lord is faithful, and He will strengthen you and guard you from the evil one.

Spirit working through the church. These teachings were meant to bring clarity and hope to the troubled believers. Through this letter, Paul aims to fortify their faith, reminding them to live with confidence and hopeful expectation for a glorious future despite present tribulations.

**Personal Notes:**

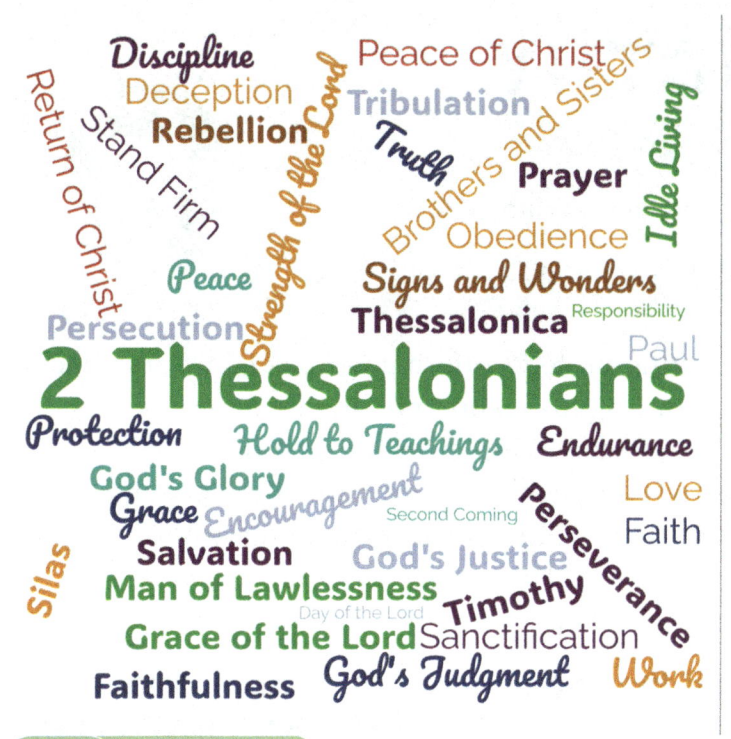

# Reflections on 2 Thessalonians
*Perseverance and Judgment*

Believers are encouraged to endure through adversities until the return of Christ. They should approach speculative claims about the timing of His return with caution. Christ's second coming will herald a period of significant judgment and reward. While awaiting Christ's return, believers are called to conduct themselves responsibly in their everyday affairs within this world.

## NOTABLE & POPULAR

**People**

Paul, Silas, Timothy

**Places**

Thessalonica, Corinth (where written)

**Events**

Clarification on the Second Coming, Encouragement

**Verses**

**2 Thessalonians 1:6-7** After all, it is only right for God to repay with affliction those who afflict you, and to grant relief to you who are oppressed and to us as well. This will take place when the Lord Jesus is revealed from heaven with His mighty angels

**2 Thessalonians 2:16-17** Now may our Lord Jesus Christ Himself and God our Father, who by grace has loved us and given us eternal comfort and good hope, encourage your hearts and strengthen you in every good word and deed.

**2 Thessalonians 3:10** For even while we were with you, we gave you this command: "If anyone is unwilling to work, he shall not eat."

# 1 TIMOTHY

**Author:** Paul

**Time Written:** Likely between 64 and 67 A.D.

**Time Covered:** Around 63 A.D.

Paul, the seasoned apostle, writes to Timothy, his young protégé, offering words of encouragement, godly guidance, and affirmation. Paul met Timothy during his second missionary journey (Acts 16:1-3) and quickly enlisted him for his mission work. Recognizing the heavy responsibility Timothy holds as the pastor of the church at Ephesus, Paul seeks to equip him with wisdom and spiritual strength. He believes that with God's help, young Timothy can surmount the daunting challenges of leading the early church. In this heartfelt letter, Paul details essential tasks for Timothy: correcting false doctrine, inspiring godly worship, and cultivating mature leadership. He

**A Key Verse:** 1 Timothy 6:12, Fight the good fight of the faith. Take hold of the eternal life to which you were called when you made the good confession before many witnesses.

also speaks candidly about the conduct required of a minister, advising Timothy to avoid false teachers and guard against greedy motives. Paul emphasizes the virtues Timothy should embody, such as righteousness, godliness, faith, love, perseverance, and gentleness. A particularly urgent warning is given against the dangers of materialism. Paul condemns the notion that godliness is a means to personal gain and stresses the importance of contentment with basic necessities. Central to Paul's message is the caution against the love of money, described as "the root of all kinds of evil" (1 Tim. 6:10). He warns that pursuing wealth can lead believers astray, resulting in spiritual ruin

**A Popular Verse:** 1 Timothy 4:12, Let no one despise your youth, but set an example for the believers in speech, in conduct, in love, in faith, in purity.

and profound sorrow. Alongside these admonitions, Paul offers majestic descriptions of God, calling Him "the King eternal, immortal, and invisible" (1 Tim. 1:17) and "the blessed and only Sovereign One—the King of kings and Lord of lords" (1 Tim. 6:15). These profound spiritually learned insights are meant to strengthen Timothy's faith and underscore the majesty and sovereignty of God. The letter, known as "First Timothy," is a timeless exhortation from a seasoned apostle to a young pastor, encouraging devoted faith and diligent service.

**Personal Notes:**

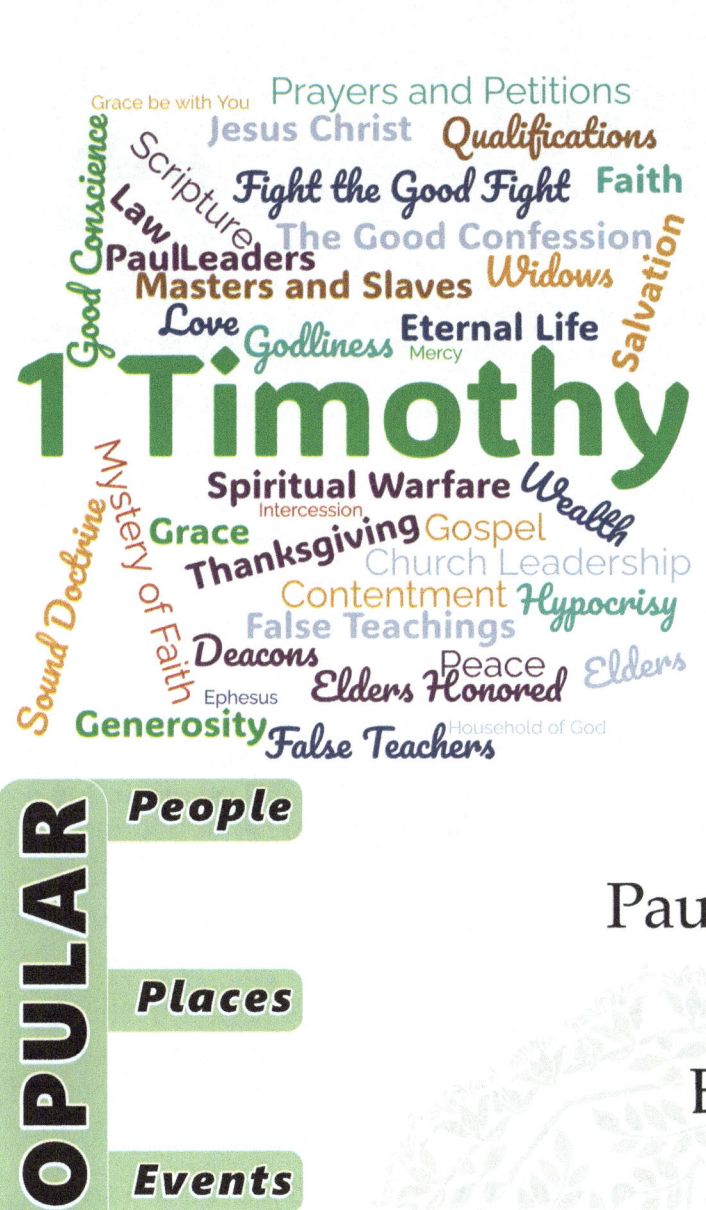

# Reflections on 1 Timothy
*Church Leadership*

The Church must serve as a stronghold against false teachings. The spread of legalistic doctrines leads individuals away from the true Gospel. It's essential to maintain a well-defined order in worship and Church authority. Different groups within the Church should address specific needs. The ministry of the Gospel should remain untainted by greed and the pursuit of monetary gain.

## NOTABLE & POPULAR

**People**

Paul, Timothy

**Places**

Ephesus

**Events**

Church Leadership Instructions, Personal Exhortations

**Verses**

**1 Timothy 2:5** For there is one God, and there is one mediator between God and men, the man Christ Jesus,

**1 Timothy 3:1-3** This is a trustworthy saying: If anyone aspires to be an overseer, he desires a noble task. An overseer, then, must be above reproach, the husband of but one wife, temperate, self-controlled, respectable, hospitable, able to teach, not dependent on wine, not violent but gentle, peaceable, and free of the love of money.

**1 Timothy 4:9-10** This is a trustworthy saying, worthy of full acceptance. To this end we labor and strive, because we have set our hope on the living God, who is the Savior of everyone, and especially of those who believe.

129

# 2 TIMOTHY

**Author:** Paul

**Time Written:** Around 67 A.D.

**Time Covered:** Around 67 A.D.

Paul's second letter to Timothy holds a unique position among his epistles as it originates from a Roman prison. Despite his confinement, Paul's words are replete with love and encouragement for Timothy, whom he regards with deep affection and spiritual concern. Paul's personal circumstances underscore a sense of urgency and intimacy, as he is acutely aware that his departure is nearing. He underscores Timothy's spiritual heritage and responsibilities, emphasizing the importance of perseverance whether in roles analogous to a soldier, athlete, farmer, or minister of Christ. In this heartfelt letter, Paul distinctly warns Timothy of impending challenges. He teaches that sound

**A Key Verse:** 2 Timothy 4:7-8, I have fought the good fight, I have finished the race, I have kept the faith. From now on there is laid up for me the crown of righteousness, which the Lord, the righteous Judge, will award to me on that day—and not only to me, but to all who crave His appearing.

doctrine will come under attack, predicting that some will abandon the truth for teachings that satisfy personal desires. Paul, however, reassures Timothy to rely on his example and the strength derived from God's Word to navigate both opposition and opportunities ahead. This epistle is punctuated with personal anecdotes reflecting Paul's sense of isolation—mentioning those like Demas who have abandoned him, and others separated by various circumstances—revealing his deep need for companionship and support as he faces his final days. The central message of Second Timothy revolves around the vigilance against false teachings and the unwavering commitment to

**A Popular Verse:** 2 Timothy 3:16, All Scripture is God-breathed and is useful for instruction, for conviction, for correction, and for training in righteousness,

truth. Paul passionately appeals to Timothy to remain diligent and to uphold the gospel amidst adversity. His call to "come before winter" reflects the urgency and importance of fellowship in the Christian journey, reminding us that even the most devout require the support of a robust faith community. Through Paul's intimate counsel and steadfast faith, readers are encouraged to cling to sound doctrine and persevere in the teachings of Christ.

**Personal Notes:**

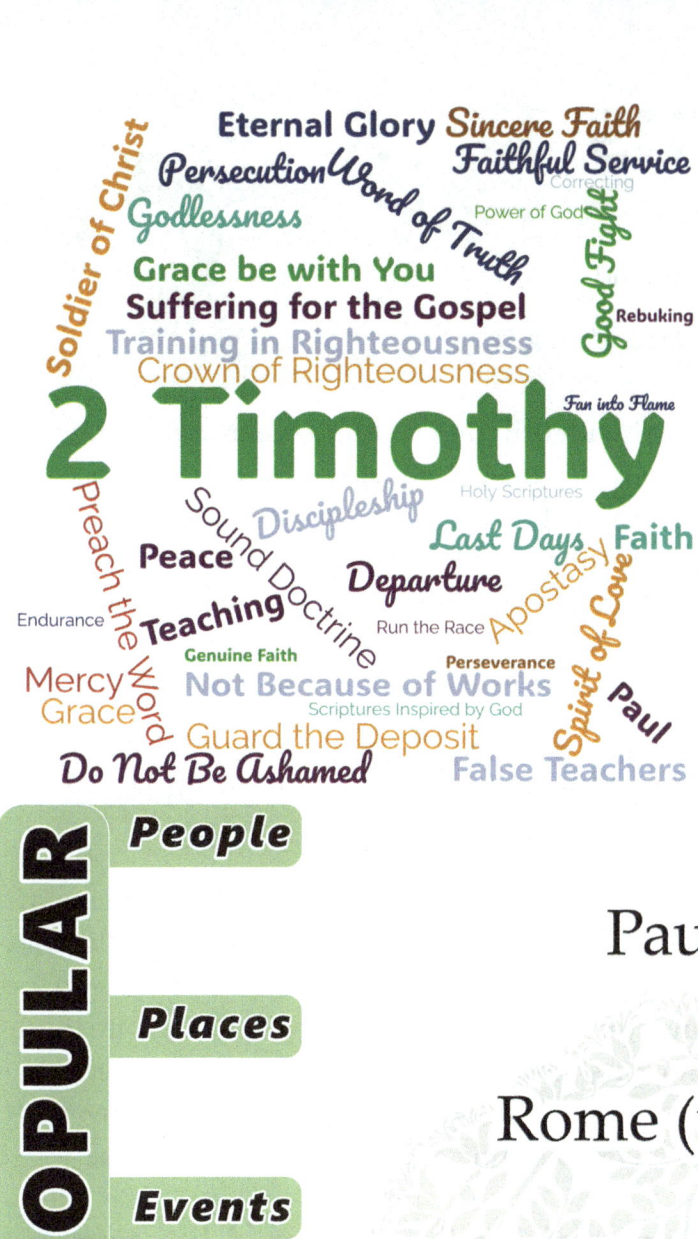

# Reflections on 2 Timothy
*Faithful Ministry*

False teachers continually challenge the Church. Church leaders are called to display courage in confronting these false influences. Leadership should derive principles and guidance from Scripture. While God promises safety to His true believers, judgment is reserved for others within the Church.

## NOTABLE & POPULAR

**People**

Paul, Timothy

**Places**

Rome (where written)

**Events**

Paul's Farewell, Faithfulness, Perseverance

**Verses**

**2 Timothy 1:7** For God has not given us a spirit of fear, but of power, love, and self-control.

**2 Timothy 1:9** He has saved us and called us to a holy calling, not because of our works, but by His own purpose and by the grace He granted us in Christ Jesus before time began.

**2 Timothy 2:15** Make every effort to present yourself approved to God, an unashamed workman who accurately handles the word of truth.

**2 Timothy 4:2** Preach the word; be prepared in season and out of season; reprove, rebuke, and encourage with every form of patient instruction.

# TITUS

**Author:** Paul

**Time Written:** Around 66 A.D.

**Time Covered:** Around 66 A.D.

*Titus – New Testament*

*Pauline Epistles – Books 6 - 18*

Paul's letter to Titus finds Titus, a young pastor, tasked with bringing order to the troubled church in Crete. This community was not only disorganized but also deeply affected by the immoral tendencies of the Cretan culture. Paul instructed Titus to establish elders of proven spiritual integrity to lead the church, so Titus could eventually reunite with Paul in Nicopolis. Paul's counsel to Titus emphasized the need for all members of the church—regardless of age or gender—to live out their professed faith in practical, everyday ways. He urged for spiritual excellence through a life marked by good deeds and admirable conduct. The content of Paul's letter is rich with guidance for

**A Key Verse:** Titus 3:5, He saved us, not by the righteous deeds we had done, but according to His mercy, through the washing of new birth and renewal by the Holy Spirit.

the Christian community in Crete. He pointed out the Cretans' notorious reputation, referencing a local saying, "Cretans are always liars, evil beasts, lazy gluttons," and Paul affirmed this to illustrate the challenges ahead (Titus 1:12-13). He cautioned Titus to be wary of those who claim to know God but deny Him by their actions, being disobedient and unfit for any good work (v. 16). Despite these daunting characterizations, Paul did not advocate for harsh measures or condemnation. Instead, he implored Titus to steer the believers towards righteous living through the transformative power of God's grace. The central message of Titus is a beautiful expounding of the practical way of the

**A Popular Verse:** Titus 2:11, For the grace of God has appeared, bringing salvation to everyone.

working out of salvation in believers' lives. Paul passionately conveyed that it is God's grace that teaches us to reject ungodliness and worldly desires, guiding us to live sensible, upright, and godly lives in the present age (Titus 2:11-12). Jesus Christ's sacrifice was not just for salvation but to purify a people dedicated to good works (v. 14). This letter sheds light on how grace, not coercion, is the key to genuine transformation, urging believers to honor and please God through their everyday actions.

**Personal Notes:**

# Reflections on Titus
*Sound Doctrine*

The Church must maintain an organized structure, led by qualified individuals. There is a collective responsibility to oppose false teachers. Specific groups within the Church have particular responsibilities, while certain general duties are shared by all believers. Underlying all Christian conduct should be God's redeeming work through Christ.

## NOTABLE & POPULAR

**People:** Paul, Titus

**Places:** Crete

**Events:** Church Order, Sound Doctrine, Good Works

**Verses:**

**Titus 1:16** They profess to know God, but by their actions they deny Him. They are detestable, disobedient, and unfit for any good deed.

**Titus 2:15** Speak these things as you encourage and rebuke with all authority. Let no one despise you.

**Titus 3:3-6** For at one time we too were foolish, disobedient, misled, and enslaved to all sorts of desires and pleasures—living in malice and envy, being hated and hating one another. But when the kindness of God our Savior and His love for mankind appeared, He saved us, not by the righteous deeds we had done, but according to His mercy, through the washing of new birth and renewal by the Holy Spirit. This is the Spirit He poured out on us abundantly through Jesus Christ our Savior,

# PHILEMON

**Author:** Paul

**Time Written:** Likely around 62 A.D.

**Time Covered:** Around 62 A.D.

The Book of Philemon is a heartfelt letter written by the Apostle Paul while he was imprisoned in Rome. Addressed to Philemon, a prominent believer who likely hosted a house church in Colossae, this epistle is unique in its deeply personal and compassionate tone. Paul writes on behalf of Onesimus, a runaway slave and thief who, through Paul's ministry, has become a devoted follower of Christ. Paul appeals to Philemon not just as a fellow believer, but as a dear brother and friend, urging him to show extraordinary Christian love and forgiveness. Within this short letter, Paul skillfully navigates the complex social dynamics of a slave returning to his master. Instead of

**A Key Verse:** Philemon 1:16, no longer as a slave, but better than a slave, as a beloved brother. He is especially beloved to me, but even more so to you, both in person and in the Lord.

advocating for harsh punishment, which was customary for runaway slaves, Paul gently persuades Philemon to welcome Onesimus back as he would Paul himself. He highlights the transformative power of the Gospel, emphasizing that Onesimus is now a brother in Christ and deserves to be treated with the same grace and love that Philemon would extend to Paul. This act of forgiveness and acceptance would not only restore Onesimus but also serve as a powerful testimony to the redemptive love of Jesus. The central theme of Philemon is the Christian duty to forgive and restore one another, reflecting the forgiveness we ourselves have received from Christ. Paul's letter is a

**A Popular Verse:** Philemon 1:6, I pray that your partnership in the faith may become effective as you fully acknowledge every good thing that is ours in Christ.

profound reminder that in God's family, social barriers are transcended, and every believer is a fellow heir to God's grace. By asking Philemon to forgive and reconcile with Onesimus, Paul underscores the transformative impact of Christian love and the importance of living out that love, even in challenging circumstances, to glorify the Lord Jesus.

**Personal Notes:**

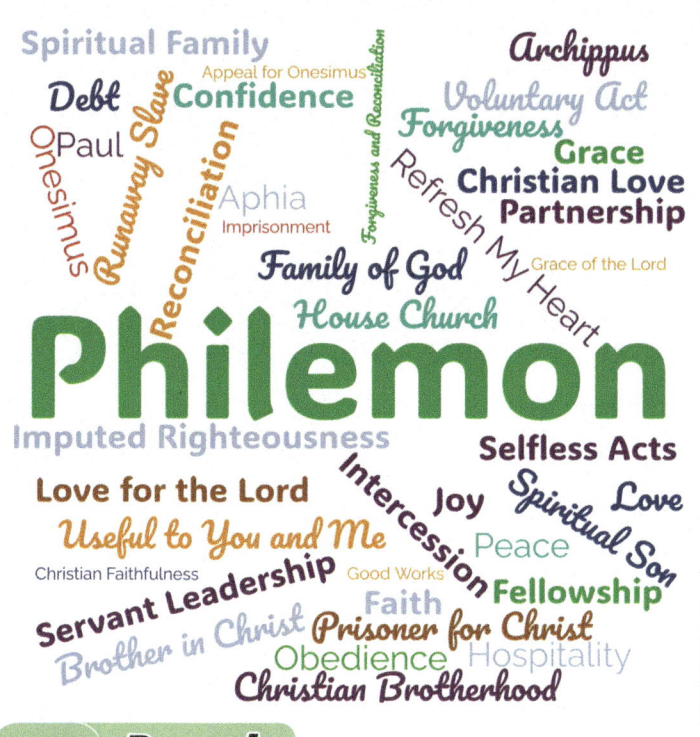

# Reflections on Philemon
*Christian Brotherhood*

Expressions of love and forgiveness are foundational in Christian interactions, as demonstrated by Paul's appeal to Philemon to welcome his runaway slave, Onesimus, as a brother in Christ, emphasizing voluntary forgiveness and reconciliation. Similarly, obedience in the Christian life should be given willingly, not out of coercion. Such acts embody the true spirit of Christian love and unity.

## NOTABLE & POPULAR

**People**

Paul, Philemon, Onesimus

**Places**

Colossae

**Events**

Appeal for Onesimus

**Verses**

**Philemon 1:4** I always thank my God, remembering you in my prayers,

**Philemon 1:7** I take great joy and encouragement in your love, because you, brother, have refreshed the hearts of the saints.

**Philemon 1:10** I appeal to you for my child Onesimus, whose father I became while I was in chains.

**Philemon 1:12** I am sending back to you him who is my very heart.

**Philemon 1:18** But if he has wronged you in any way or owes you anything, charge it to my account.

# GENERAL EPISTLES

## General Epistles

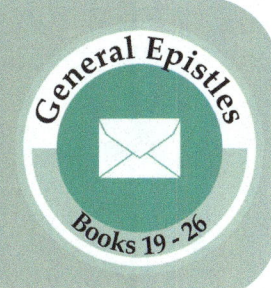

**James** ³ **John** **Hebrews**
**General** ² **Peter** **Epistles**
**1 Peter** Jude **2 John** **1 John**

The general epistles, penned by apostles Peter, John, James (the brother of Jesus), and Jude, along with the book of Hebrews whose authorship remains uncertain, collectively offer profound insights into the Christian faith. While some suggest Paul might have written Hebrews, its true author is still unknown. These epistles address pressing issues of faith, practical living, and the challenges posed by false teachers. James, in particular, emphasizes the importance of practical Christian living, encouraging believers to demonstrate their faith through deeds.

Within these writings, there is a recurring theme concerning the authenticity of faith and the perils of false teachings. For instance, the epistles from Peter, John, and Jude focus on distinguishing true faith from fraudulent doctrines, providing believers with ways to identify and counteract deceptive teachings. They highlight the importance of holding fast to the apostolic teachings, remaining vigilant, and living a life that reflects genuine commitment to Christ.

Moreover, Peter and Jude specifically address the theme of suffering, urging believers to remain steadfast and faithful amidst trials and persecution. They affirm that suffering for one's faith is part and parcel of the Christian journey and offer encouragement and hope to persevere. By stressing these themes, the general epistles fortify the early church and modern believers against both internal and external challenges, ensuring that the faith handed down from the apostles remains pure and powerful. Through their admonitions and teachings, these epistles continue to provide essential guidance and hope for Christians facing various trials and temptations, fostering a robust and resilient faith community.

**Personal Notes:**

# HEBREWS

**Author:** Traditionally Paul – possibly Luke, Apollos, or Barnabas

**Time Written:** Likely before 70 A.D.

**Time Covered:** Around 68 A.D.

The Book of Hebrews addresses Jewish Christians who faced intense persecution after placing their faith in Jesus Christ as their Messiah and Savior. Fearful and contemplating a return to Judaism to avoid suffering, these believers needed encouragement. The writer of Hebrews exhorts them to "hold firmly to what we profess" (Hebrews 4:14) and to "go on to maturity" (Hebrews 6:1). Although the author remains anonymous in early manuscripts, tradition often credits Paul with the writing. The book, titled "To the Hebrews," is a profound appeal to maintain faith in Christ, emphasizing His supremacy over the old Judaic system. Hebrews masterfully outlines the

**A Key Verse:** Hebrews 10:23–24, Let us hold resolutely to the hope we profess, for He who promised is faithful. And let us consider how to spur one another on to love and good deeds.

superiority of Christ in every aspect of the Jewish faith. Jesus is greater than the angels, who worship Him. He surpasses Moses, for He is the Creator and the One who empowered Moses. Christ's priesthood exceeds that of Aaron's, as He offers Himself as an eternal, infinitely valuable sacrifice. Furthermore, Jesus mediates a superior, eternal covenant, replacing the old laws with a promise of everlasting life. The author argues that the spiritual and eternal gains found in Christ far outweigh any worldly comforts or securities one might seek by abandoning Him. At its core, Hebrews urges believers to remain confident in their faith by focusing on Jesus. The book reminds

**A Popular Verse:** Hebrews 11:1, Now faith is the assurance of what we hope for and the certainty of what we do not see.

us to "fix our eyes on Jesus, the author and perfecter of our faith," who endured immense hostility from sinners (Hebrews 12:2-3). This encouragement helps believers to avoid growing weary and discouraged, anchoring their hope in Christ's ultimate triumph and eternal rewards. The theme of the book is clear: in light of Jesus' unparalleled superiority, perseverance in Him is the path to receiving divine blessings and the fulfillment of God's promises to the faithful.

**Personal Notes:**

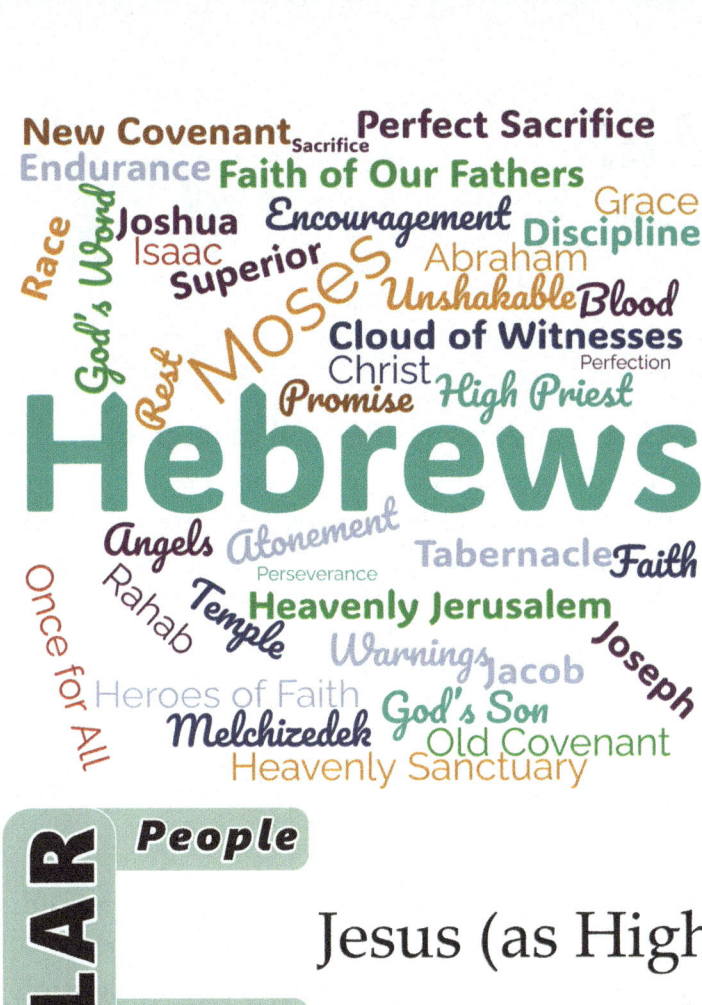

# Reflections on Hebrews
*Christ's Superiority*

Christ is exalted above angels, Moses, Aaron, and the priestly ministry of the Old Testament. The Old Testament recognized the transitional nature of its structures, so the new covenant does not contradict the old. Church members are called to endure in their faithfulness to the grace made possible by Jesus Christ, to the new covenant, waiting patiently until the end, knowing with certainty that they will fully receive all that their Lord has promised to those who believe.

## NOTABLE & POPULAR

**People**

Jesus (as High Priest), Melchizedek

**Places**

Jerusalem, the Temple (both mentioned)

**Events**

Superiority of Christ, Faith, Warnings Against Apostasy

**Verses**

**Hebrews 1:1-2** On many past occasions and in many different ways, God spoke to our fathers through the prophets. But in these last days He has spoken to us by His Son, whom He appointed heir of all things, and through whom He made the universe.

**Hebrews 2:3** how shall we escape if we neglect such a great salvation? This salvation was first announced by the Lord, was confirmed to us by those who heard Him,

**Hebrews 4:14-16** Therefore, since we have a great high priest who has passed through the heavens, Jesus the Son of God, let us hold firmly to what we profess. For we do not have a high priest who is unable to sympathize with our weaknesses, but we have one who was tempted in every way that we are, yet was without sin. Let us then approach the throne of grace with confidence, so that we may receive mercy and find grace to help us in our time of need.

# JAMES

**Author:** James

**Time Written:** Likely around 50 A.D.

**Time Covered:** 45 A.D.

The Book of James, attributed to James, the brother of Jesus, underscores the vital connection between faith and works. James candidly states, "faith without works is dead" (James 2:26), emphasizing that mere verbal or mental assent is insufficient. True faith must express itself through visible, godly actions. Throughout this practical epistle, James integrates faith with daily life, urging believers to demonstrate their faith through deeds that reflect the reality of their trust in God. A faith that does not result in action is not faith at all, but a mere shadow, ineffective and lifeless. James highlights several characteristics of genuine faith. True faith endures trials, fostering

**A Key Verse:** James 2:17, So too, faith by itself, if it does not result in action, is dead.

perseverance and maturity. It understands temptations, resisting the lure of sin through the power granted by Christ's sacrifice and resurrection. James also makes it clear that genuine faith harbors no prejudice, reflecting the inclusive love God has for every person. Additionally, true faith controls the tongue, recognizing the immense power of words and seeking to use them to uplift and encourage others. Moreover, genuine faith chooses heavenly wisdom over earthly wisdom, leading to a life that aligns with God's will and purposes. Ultimately, the theme of James is that real faith is active and transformative. Genuine faith separates believers from worldly influences and draws

**A Popular Verse:** James 1:2-3, Consider it pure joy, my brothers, when you encounter trials of many kinds, because you know that the testing of your faith develops perseverance.

them closer to God, enabling resistance to the devil and fostering humility. This faith waits patiently for the return of the Lord, sustaining believers through trials without complaint. Genuine faith is dynamic, shaping daily actions and decisions by relying on God's infinite power. This letter, or "Epistle" of James reminds us that living faith is evident in lives marked by active obedience and wholehearted trust in God.

**Personal Notes:**

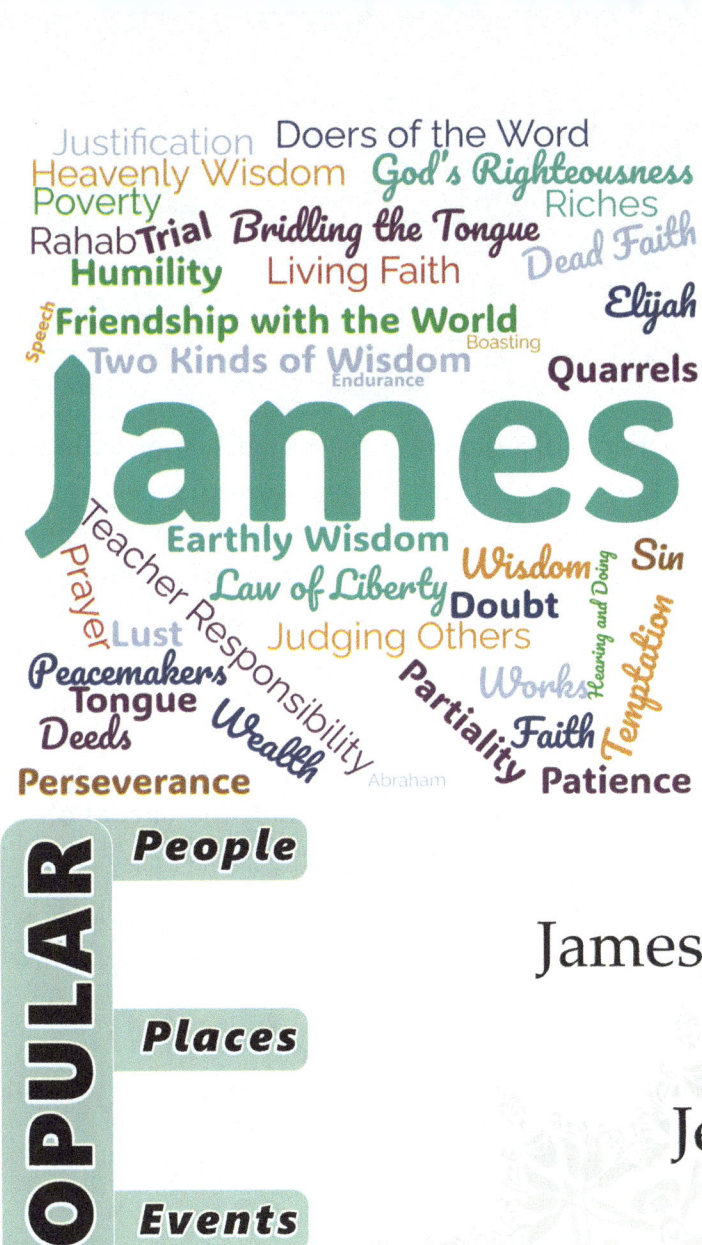

## Reflections on James
*Faith in Action*

Believers are encouraged to seek wisdom from God to help them remain faithful amidst trials and conflicts. It is crucial that hearing God's Word leads to putting it into practice. Genuine saving faith is demonstrated through good deeds, especially in caring for the less fortunate. Divine wisdom guides believers in loving and serving one another. Maintaining harmony within the Christian community is of utmost importance.

## NOTABLE & POPULAR

**People**

James, the Brethren

**Places**

Jerusalem

**Events**

Faith and Works, Wisdom, Rich and Poor, Taming the Tongue

**Verses**

**James 1:19** My beloved brothers, understand this: Everyone should be quick to listen, slow to speak, and slow to anger,

**James 2:18** But someone will say, "You have faith and I have deeds." Show me your faith without deeds, and I will show you my faith by my deeds.

**James 3:5** In the same way, the tongue is a small part of the body, but it boasts of great things. Consider how small a spark sets a great forest ablaze.

**James 5:16** Therefore confess your sins to each other and pray for each other so that you may be healed. The prayer of a righteous man has great power to prevail.

141

# 1 PETER

**Author:** Peter

**Time Written:** Likely around 64 A.D.

**Time Covered:** Around 64 A.D.

Persecution can lead to growth or bitterness in a Christian's life, depending on their response. In his first letter, Peter encourages believers facing persecution to conduct themselves courageously for Christ. Being born again to a living hope, they are called to imitate the Holy One and maintain their character and conduct above reproach. Peter emphasizes living in godliness, honor, and humble submission: citizens toward government, servants toward masters, wives toward husbands, husbands toward wives, and Christians toward one another. After explaining the meaning of submission, he addresses adversity, urging persecuted Christians not to be surprised by trials but to

**A Key Verse:** 1 Peter 2:9, But you are a chosen people, a royal priesthood, a holy nation, a people for God's own possession, to proclaim the virtues of Him who called you out of darkness into His marvelous light.

rejoice in sharing Christ's sufferings. Peter's letter was written to Christians in northern Asia Minor who were enduring severe persecution for their faith. He wanted to remind them that facing opposition is part of following Christ, as Jesus Himself experienced suffering. Christians are encouraged to find hope and joy in being counted worthy to suffer for His name, as seen in Acts 5:41. Peter assures them that those who commit their souls to God and continue doing good, even in suffering, will endure and glorify God. Rather than fearing trials, believers are to see them as opportunities to partake in Christ's sufferings and to anticipate the joy of His future glory. The

**A Popular Verse:** 1 Peter 5:7, Cast all your anxiety on Him, because He cares for you.

central theme of 1 Peter is that suffering is an integral part of walking with and serving Jesus Christ. This suffering should not be feared but embraced. In the original Greek in which it was written, Peter opens his epistle with "Petros apostolos Jesou Christou," which means "Peter, the apostle of Jesus Christ," forming the early title "Petrou A" or "First of Peter." Through this heartfelt message, Peter encourages believers to persevere in faith, enduring trials with a spirit of rejoicing, knowing that their willingness to do so brings glory to God and will ultimately lead to shared glory with Christ.

**Personal Notes:**

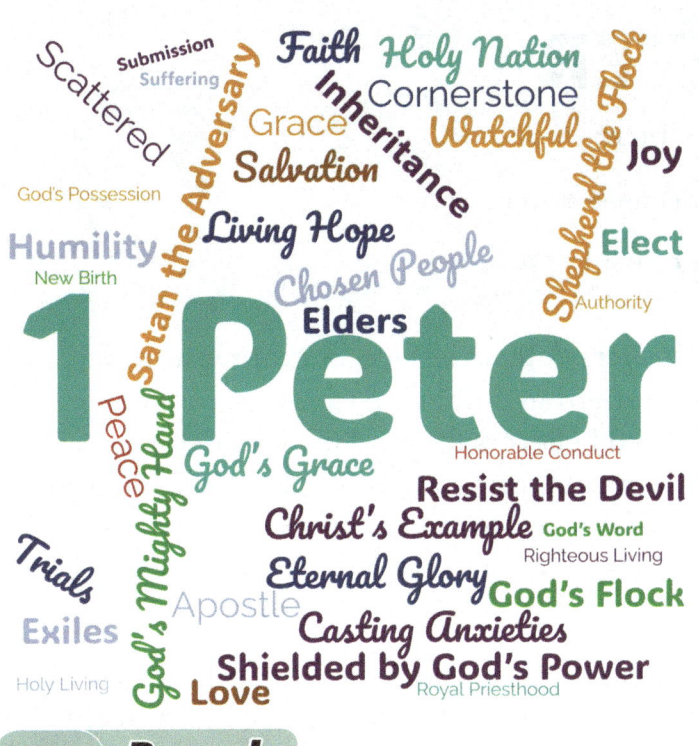

# Reflections on 1 Peter
*Suffering and Glory*

Christians are granted the immense privilege of witnessing God's grand salvation through Christ. With this privilege comes a set of crucial responsibilities. Christians are called to pursue holiness, to love each other earnestly, and to dedicate themselves to the glory of God. Relationships, both within and outside the Church, should align with the standards set by Christ, as opposed to worldly standards. When facing suffering, Christians should maintain the proper perspective as disciples of Christ.

## NOTABLE & POPULAR

**People**

Peter, Silvanus (Silas), Mark

**Places**

Babylon (possibly figurative of Rome)

**Events**

Encouragement in Persecution, Christian Conduct

**Verses**

**1 Peter 1:3** Blessed be the God and Father of our Lord Jesus Christ! By His great mercy He has given us new birth into a living hope through the resurrection of Jesus Christ from the dead,

**1 Peter 2:24** He Himself bore our sins in His body on the tree, so that we might die to sin and live to righteousness. "By His stripes you are healed."

**1 Peter 5:8-9** Be sober-minded and alert. Your adversary the devil prowls around like a roaring lion, seeking someone to devour. Resist him, standing firm in your faith and in the knowledge that your brothers throughout the world are undergoing the same kinds of suffering.

# 2 PETER

**Author:** Peter

**Time Written:** Likely between 67 and 68 A.D.

**Time Covered:** Around 67 A.D.

*2 Peter — New Testament*

*General Epistles — Books 19 - 26*

In his second epistle, the Apostle Peter addresses believers with an earnest but caring warning against false teachers who seek to distort the gospel truth from within the Christian community. This letter is a follow-up to 1 Peter, wherein he bolstered believers to stand firm amidst external persecutions. In 2 Peter, his focus shifts to an internal threat, urging Christians to remain guarded against corrupt doctrines infiltrating the church. Peter calls for vigilance in nurturing personal obedience and living virtuously in alignment with God's will. Peter passionately exhorts believers to cultivate a life characterized by moral excellence, knowledge, self-control, perseverance,

**A Key Verse:** 2 Peter 1:3, His divine power has given us everything we need for life and godliness through the knowledge of Him who called us by His own glory and excellence.

godliness, brotherly kindness, and selfless love. He assures them that such dedication yields abundant blessings, citing, "For if you possess these qualities and continue to grow in them, they will keep you from being ineffective and unproductive in your knowledge of our Lord Jesus Christ" (2 Peter 1:8). Contrarily, the false teachers he condemns advocate for sensuality, arrogance, greed, and covetousness, dismissing the certainty of future judgment and indulging in present-day excesses. Peter harshly reminds the faithful that though God is loving and patient, He will ultimately judge the world, and these deceivers will "utterly perish in their own corruption; And

**A Popular Verse:** 2 Peter 3:9, The Lord is not slow in keeping His promise as some understand slowness, but is patient with you, not wanting anyone to perish but everyone to come to repentance.

shall receive the reward of unrighteousness" (2 Peter 2:12-13). The central theme of 2 Peter is clear: Despite the seductive allure of false teachings that cater to the flesh, such doctrines lead to dire consequences under God's righteous judgment. Peter emphasizes the urgency of remembering Christ's impending return, which will bring both judgment and rewards. This anticipation should inspire believers to live godly, blameless, and committed lives. The letter, known in Greek as Petro B to distinguish it from the first epistle, continues to underscore that embracing falsehood results in ultimate destruction, whereas true adherence to the faith secures divine blessings and eternal rewards.

**Personal Notes:**

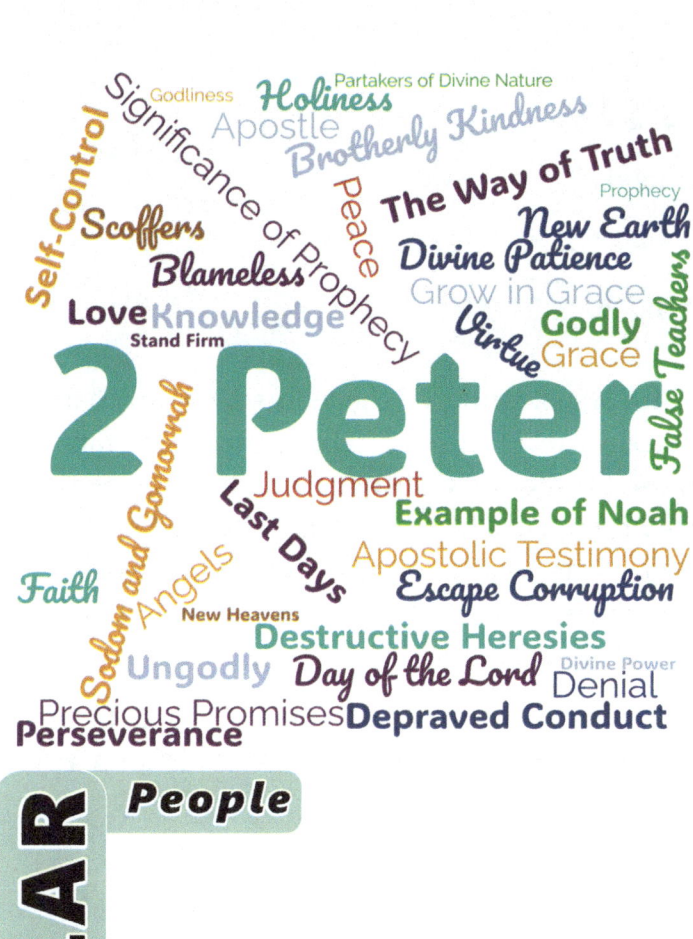

# Reflections on 2 Peter
*False Teachers*

Due to their immense blessings in Christ, Christians should continually pursue spiritual growth. The certainty of Christ's return is confirmed by eyewitnesses and Scripture. False teachers who deny Christ's return will face severe divine judgment. The delay in Jesus's return reflects God's patience towards His people. While Christians are called to be patient, they should also endeavor to hasten the day of Christ's return through prayer, obedience, and evangelism.

## NOTABLE & POPULAR

**People**

Peter

**Places**

Unspecified, likely written from Rome

**Events**

Warnings Against False Teachers, Day of the Lord

**Verses**

**2 Peter 1:16** For we did not follow cleverly devised fables when we made known to you the power and coming of our Lord Jesus Christ, but we were eyewitnesses of His majesty.

**2 Peter 1:20** Above all, you must understand that no prophecy of Scripture comes from one's own interpretation.

**2 Peter 2:1** Now there were also false prophets among the people, just as there will be false teachers among you. They will secretly introduce destructive heresies, even denying the Master who bought them—bringing swift destruction on themselves.

**2 Peter 3:8** Beloved, do not let this one thing escape your notice: With the Lord a day is like a thousand years, and a thousand years are like a day.

# 1 JOHN

**Author:** John

**Time Written:** Likely between 90 and 95 A.D.

**Time Covered:** Around 90 to 94 A.D.

The Apostle John, known for his deep relationship with Jesus, authored the letters recognized as 1 John, 2 John, and 3 John. These epistles were written during a time when the early church faced severe challenges from false teachers, particularly those promoting Gnostic beliefs, such as, secret mystical knowledge available only to a few believers, and bizarre ideas such as 'Jesus did not have a real physical body'... just to name a few. John's purpose was to remind the believers of the core principles of their faith and to encourage them to remain steadfast in their fellowship with God. His letters, though not signed with his name, have been traditionally ascribed to him due to their

**A Key Verse:** 1 John 4:10, And love consists in this: not that we loved God, but that He loved us and sent His Son as the atoning sacrifice for our sins.

intimate tone and consistent themes. In 1 John, he provides a rich exposition on the nature of God being light, love, and life. He emphasizes that true fellowship with God requires walking in His light, which necessitates personal holiness and truthfulness. John urges the believers to confess their sins continually so that Jesus' sacrificial blood can purify them. In 2 John, the apostle cautions the "elect lady and her children" to practice discernment in their relationships. He advises them against offering hospitality to false teachers who deny the incarnation of Christ. In 3 John, he commends Gaius for his faithful hospitality towards missionaries and reprimands Diotrephes for his divisive

**A Popular Verse:** 1 John 4:7-8, Beloved, let us love one another, because love comes from God. Everyone who loves has been born of God and knows God. Whoever does not love does not know God, because God is love.

and prideful behavior. The core theme binding these letters is rooted in the character of God as love. To truly know God is to embody His 'agape' love (a Greek word meaning a selfless, unconditional, or sacrificial kind of love) as we interact with others. John insists that this love is not merely an emotion but must be demonstrated through actions of genuine kindness and forgiveness. Alongside love, John stresses the importance of adhering to divine truth, as he reminds believers of the significance of Jesus Christ's sacrifice. By adhering to these principles, believers can navigate the perils of false teachings and remain committed to their faith.

**Personal Notes:**

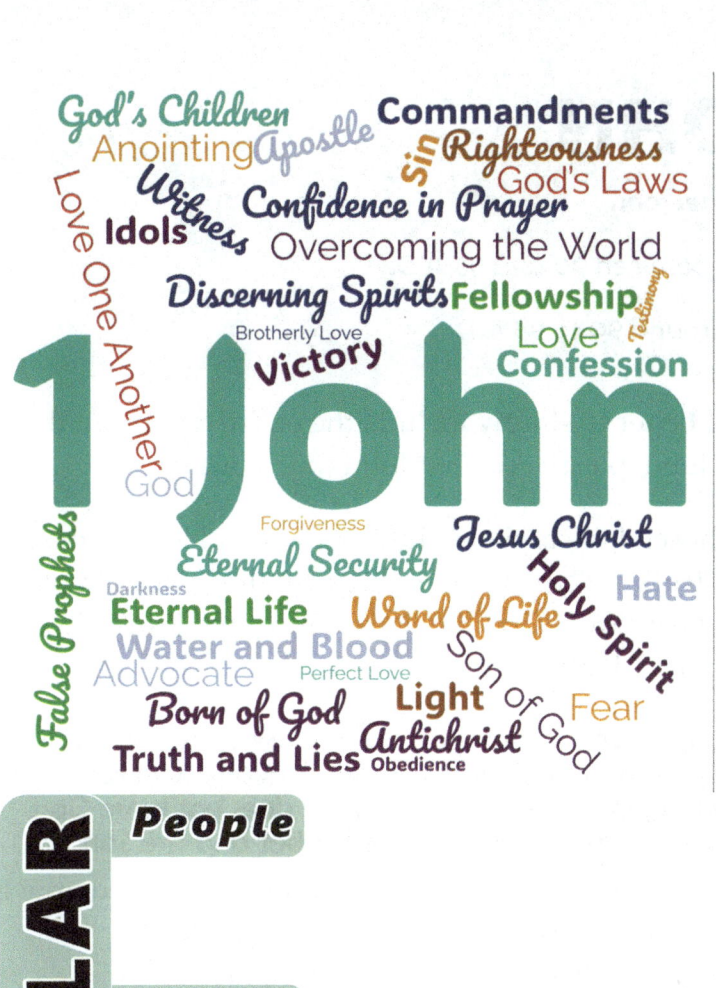

# Reflections on 1 John
*Love and Fellowship*

Salvation received from God ignites a life of righteousness, especially nurturing love for fellow believers. Christ took on full human form. Not everyone who professes to follow Christ is a genuine disciple. Believers are encouraged to examine themselves to ensure the authenticity of their faith in Christ. Those who truly love God and whose lives reflect a commitment to living for Christ can confidently have full assurance of their salvation.

## NOTABLE & POPULAR

**People**

John

**Places**

Likely from Ephesus

**Events**

God is Light, Love, Assurance

**Verses**

**1 John 1:9** If we confess our sins, He is faithful and just to forgive us our sins and to cleanse us from all unrighteousness.

**1 John 3:6** No one who remains in Him keeps on sinning. No one who continues to sin has seen Him or known Him.

**1 John 4:4** You, little children, are from God and have overcome them, because greater is He who is in you than he who is in the world.

**1 John 5:13** I have written these things to you who believe in the name of the Son of God, so that you may know that you have eternal life.

# 2 JOHN

**Author:** John

**Time Written:** Likely between 90 and 95 A.D.

**Time Covered:** Around 90 to 94 A.D.

**NOTE**: Because of the brevity of 2 John, it seemed better to simply include the entire text (from the BSB - Berean Standard Bible). For comments on 2 John, please see First John (one page back).

**A Greeting from the Elder** (1) The elder, To the chosen lady and her children, whom I love in the truth—and not I alone, but also all who know the truth— (2) because of the truth that abides in us and will be with us forever: (3) Grace, mercy, and peace from God the Father and from Jesus Christ, the Son of the Father, will be with us in truth and love. **Walking in the Truth** (4) I was overjoyed to

> **A Key Verse:** 2 John 1:8–9, Watch yourselves, so that you do not lose what we have worked for, but that you may be fully rewarded. Anyone who runs ahead without remaining in the teaching of Christ does not have God. Whoever remains in His teaching has both the Father and the Son.

find some of your children walking in the truth, just as the Father has commanded us. (5) And now I urge you, dear lady—not as a new commandment to you, but one we have had from the beginning—that we love one another. (6) And this is love, that we walk according to His commandments. This is the very commandment you have heard from the beginning, that you must walk in love. **Beware of Deceivers,** (7) For many deceivers have gone out into the world, refusing to confess the coming of Jesus Christ in the flesh. Any such person is the deceiver and the Antichrist. (8) Watch yourselves, so that you do not lose what we have worked for, but that you may be fully

> **A Popular Verse:** 2 John 1:6, And this is love, that we walk according to His commandments. This is the very commandment you have heard from the beginning, that you must walk in love.

rewarded. (9) Anyone who runs ahead without remaining in the teaching of Christ does not have God. Whoever remains in His teaching has both the Father and the Son. (10) If anyone comes to you but does not bring this teaching, do not receive him into your home or even greet him. (11) Whoever greets such a person shares in his evil deeds. **Conclusion** (12) I have many things to write to you, but I would prefer not to do so with paper and ink. Instead, I hope to come and speak with you face to face, so that our joy may be complete. (13) The children of your elect sister send you greetings.

**Personal Notes:**

# Reflections on 2 John
*Truth and Love*

Within the Christian community, love is the cornerstone of moral responsibility for Christ's followers. Denying the full incarnation of Christ is 'deceptive' and "antichrist." Those who believe in Jesus should be careful to guard against such deceptions and have no part of them.

## NOTABLE & POPULAR

**People**

John, the "elect lady" and her children

**Places**

Likely from Ephesus

**Events**

Walking in Truth, Warning Against Deceivers

**Verses**

**2 John 1:3** Grace, mercy, and peace from God the Father and from Jesus Christ, the Son of the Father, will be with us in truth and love.

**2 John 1:5** And now I urge you, dear lady—not as a new commandment to you, but one we have had from the beginning—that we love one another.

**2 John 1:7** For many deceivers have gone out into the world, refusing to confess the coming of Jesus Christ in the flesh. Any such person is the deceiver and the antichrist.

**2 John 1:12** I have many things to write to you, but I would prefer not to do so with paper and ink. Instead, I hope to come and speak with you face to face, so that our joy may be complete.

149

# 3 JOHN

**Author:** John

**Time Written:** Likely between 90 and 95 A.D.

**Time Covered:** Around 90 to 94 A.D.

*3 John — New Testament*

*General Epistles — Books 19 - 26*

**NOTE**: Because of the brevity of 3 John, it seemed better to simply include the entire text (from the BSB - Berean Standard Bible). For comments on 3 John, please see First John (two pages back).

**A Greeting from the Elder** (1) The elder, To the beloved Gaius, whom I love in the truth: (2) Beloved, I pray that in every way you may prosper and enjoy good health, as your soul also prospers. (3) For I was overjoyed when the brothers came and testified about your devotion to the truth, in which you continue to walk. (4) I have no greater joy than to hear that my children are

**A Key Verse:** 3 John 1:4, I have no greater joy than to hear that my children are walking in the truth.

walking in the truth. **Gaius Commended for Hospitality** (5) Beloved, you are faithful in what you are doing for the brothers, and especially since they are strangers to you. (6) They have testified to the church about your love. You will do well to send them on their way in a manner worthy of God. (7) For they went out on behalf of the Name, accepting nothing from the Gentiles. (8) Therefore we ought to support such men, so that we may be fellow workers for the truth. **Diotrephes and Demetrius** (9) I have written to the church about this, but Diotrephes, who loves to be first, will not accept our instruction. (10) So if I come, I will call attention to his malicious slander against us. And

**A Popular Verse:** 3 John 1:11, Beloved, do not imitate what is evil, but what is good. The one who does good is of God; the one who does evil has not seen God.

unsatisfied with that, he refuses to welcome the brothers and forbids those who want to do so, even putting them out of the church. (11) Beloved, do not imitate what is evil, but what is good. The one who does good is of God; the one who does evil has not seen God. (12) Demetrius has received a good testimony from everyone, and from the truth itself. We also testify for him, and you know that our testimony is true. **Conclusion** (13) I have many things to write to you, but I would prefer not to do so with pen and ink. (14) Instead, I hope to see you soon and speak with you face to face. Peace to you. The friends here send you greetings. Greet each of our friends there by name.

**Personal Notes:**

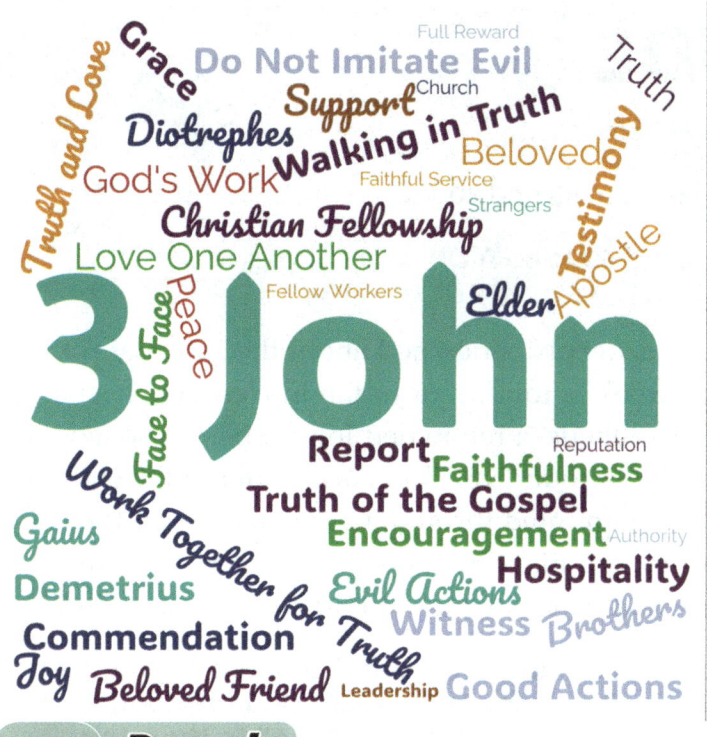

# Reflections on 3 John
*Hospitality and Truth*

Christians who consistently show kindness to others deserve commendation. Extending hospitality, especially towards ministers of the gospel, is both a significant privilege and duty for Christians. Christian leaders should cultivate a culture of appreciation and support, avoiding the instillation of fear and mistreatment among one another.

## NOTABLE & POPULAR

**People:** John, Gaius, Diotrephes, Demetrius

**Places:** Likely from Ephesus

**Events:** Hospitality, Truth, Warning Against Diotrephes

**Verses:**

3 John 1:2 Beloved, I pray that in every way you may prosper and enjoy good health, as your soul also prospers.

3 John 1:5-6 Beloved, you are faithful in what you are doing for the brothers, and especially since they are strangers to you. They have testified to the church about your love. You will do well to send them on their way in a manner worthy of God.

3 John 1:8 Therefore we ought to support such men, so that we may be fellow workers for the truth.

3 John 1:12 Demetrius has received a good testimony from everyone, and from the truth itself. We also testify for him, and you know that our testimony is true.

# JUDE

**Author:** Jude

**Time Written:** Likely between 65 and 80 A.D.

**Time Covered:** Around 60 to 80 A.D.

Jude, the author of the epistle that bears his name, was deeply concerned about the spiritual well-being of the early Christian community. Known in Greek as Ioudas, or Judah in Hebrew, this name and variations of it was popular because of Judas Maccabeus, a renowned Jewish hero who led the resistance against Syria during the Maccabean Revolt of around 167 B.C. As a leader in the church, Jude initially set out to write about the shared salvation granted through Christ. However, the rise of false teachings within the church compelled him to shift his focus, urging believers to adamantly defend the integrity of their faith. This brief yet poignant letter includes vivid reminders of God's

**A Key Verse:** Jude 1:3, Beloved, although I made every effort to write to you about the salvation we share, I felt it necessary to write and urge you to contend earnestly for the faith entrusted once for all to the saints.

judgments on unfaithful Israel, rebellious angels, and the depraved cities of Sodom and Gomorrah. Jude warns of false teachers infiltrating the congregation, distorting God's grace into a pretext for immoral behavior and denying the sovereignty of Jesus Christ. His compelling call to action is meant to rouse believers into safeguarding their faith and the Gospel's truth. Jude's writing reflects a deep pastoral concern, emphasizing the urgency of spiritual vigilance and purity in the face of deceit. The central theme of the letter encourages believers to "contend earnestly for the faith" while living in the divine love of God. Jude underscores the importance of relying on God's grace to

**A Popular Verse:** Jude 1:25, to the only God our Savior be glory, majesty, dominion, and authority through Jesus Christ our Lord before all time, and now, and for all eternity. Amen.

prevent believers from falling into sin and to present them blameless with great joy before His glory. This great spiritual struggle demands both personal commitment and communal support, reminding us that while the threat of deception is significant, God's power to preserve and protect His children is far greater. Jude's message is a strong reminder to remain steadfast in faith and truth, ever reliant on the sustenance provided by our Lord.

**Personal Notes:**

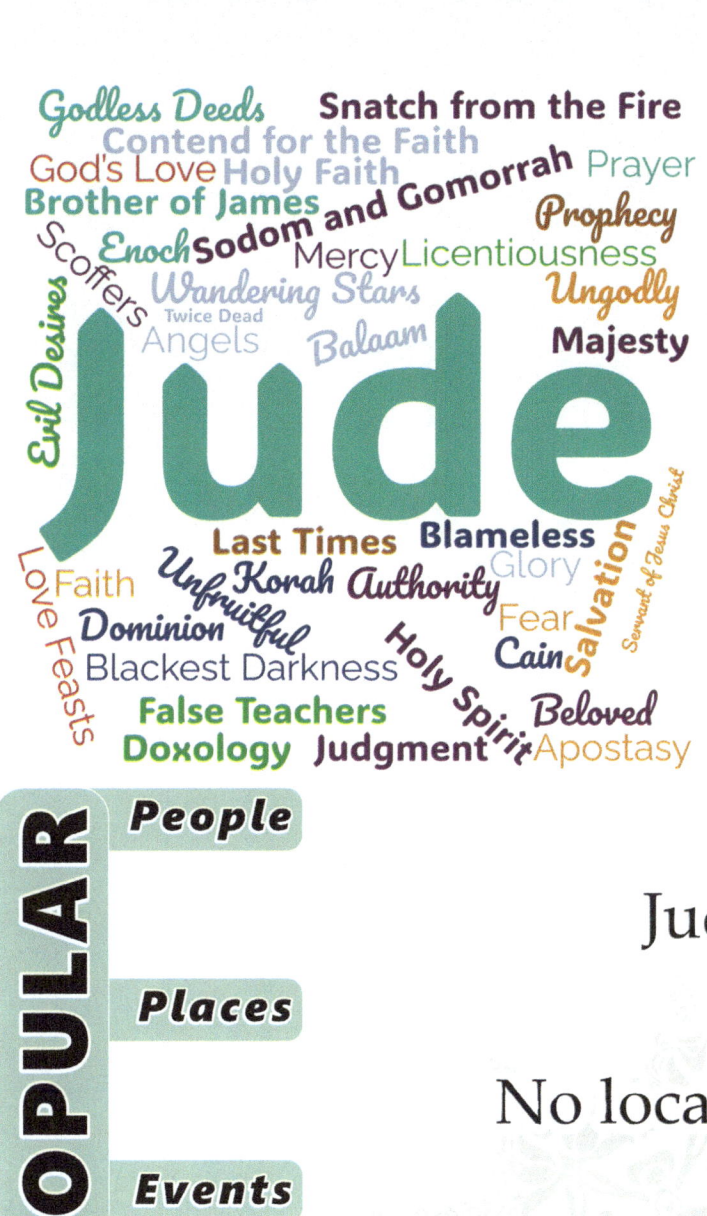

# Reflections on Jude
*Contending for Faith*

Those who defy God and Christ are destined for severe judgment. The Church must firmly resist false teachers. While Christians enjoy the liberty and free grace of God, this does not grant them a license to sin. Believers are called to actively engage in good deeds and pursue spiritual growth, fully acknowledging their responsibilities in these areas.

## Notable & Popular

**People**

Jude, James

**Places**

No locations specified

**Events**

Contending for the Faith, Judgment on False Teachers

**Verses**

**Jude 1:4** For certain men have crept in among you unnoticed—ungodly ones who were designated long ago for condemnation. They turn the grace of our God into a license for immorality, and they deny our only Master and Lord, Jesus Christ.

**Jude 1:17-19** But you, beloved, remember what was foretold by the apostles of our Lord Jesus Christ when they said to you, "In the last times there will be scoffers who will follow after their own ungodly desires." These are the ones who cause divisions, who are worldly and devoid of the Spirit.

**Jude 1:20-21** But you, beloved, by building yourselves up in your most holy faith and praying in the Holy Spirit, keep yourselves in the love of God as you await the mercy of our Lord Jesus Christ to bring you eternal life.

# PROPHETIC

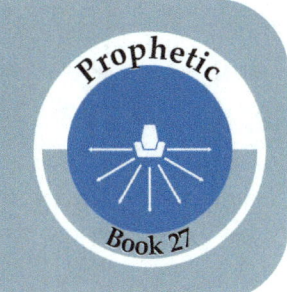

## Prophetic Revelation
*The Revelation to John* — *Apocalypse* — *Revelation of St. John the Divine*

The final book of the New Testament is Revelation, a prophetic book that unveils future events. Written by the apostle John, it is rich with vivid symbols and imagery, many of which are explained through references to the Old Testament. This extraordinary book provides a glimpse into God's ultimate plan for humanity and the world, offering both warning and hope.

Beginning in chapter 6, Revelation delves into the intense period known as the tribulation, a time of unprecedented trials and suffering. It then moves forward to describe the triumphant second coming of Christ, when He will return in glory to defeat evil. Following this, the book depicts the establishment of the millennial kingdom, a thousand-year reign of Christ on earth characterized by peace and righteousness.

Revelation concludes by portraying the final judgment, where the destinies of all people are eternally sealed. Ultimately, it reveals the new creation and the eternal state, where believers will live in God's presence forever. Through its powerful visions and messages, the book of Revelation encourages Christians to remain faithful and resolute, offering assurance that, despite present struggles, God's victory and the hope of eternal life are certain.

**Personal Notes:**

# REVELATION

**Author:** John

**Time Written:** Around 95 A.D

**Time Covered:** Likely 95 A.D.

Just as Genesis begins the narrative of creation and humanity, Revelation brings the divine story to its majestic conclusion. In this final book, God completes His redemptive purposes and stands vindicated before all creation. While prophecies are present throughout the New Testament, Revelation uniquely focuses on future events. Heavily borrowing symbols and imagery from the Old Testament, particularly from the Book of Daniel, Revelation challenges readers to discern between literal and symbolic language, often confounding even seasoned scholars. Revelation's structure includes several profound moments of worship where heavenly beings and the saints of

**A Key Verse:** Revelation 7:16, 'Never again will they hunger, and never will they thirst; nor will the sun beat down upon them, nor any scorching heat.'

God exalt His holy character and just judgments. These high points are frequently depicted as joyous songs of praise and worship. The Greek title, *Apokalypsis Ioannou*, translates to "Revelation of John" or "Apocalypse," meaning an unveiling or disclosure. The first verse refers to it as the "Revelation of Jesus Christ," indicating it is both from Christ and about Him, revealing truth that would otherwise remain hidden. Originally addressed to seven churches in Asia Minor, which is modern-day Turkey, the message of Revelation extends to all believers. It serves to inspire Christians with the hope of Christ's return in powerful glory, motivating believers to Spirit-filled

**A Popular Verse:** Revelation 7:17, For the Lamb in the center of the throne will be their shepherd. 'He will lead them to springs of living water,' and 'God will wipe away every tear from their eyes.' "

and loving actions, both for Him and because of Him. Central to Revelation are the awe-inspiring visions and symbols of the resurrected Christ. He alone wields the authority to judge, remake, and rule the earth in righteousness. The book encourages believers to live with the anticipation of God's ultimate victory, urging unwavering faithfulness and stewardship in light of Christ's imminent return.

**Personal Notes:**

## Reflections on Revelation
*Ultimate Victory*

In this sin-stricken world, the Church endures much suffering. God requires sincere repentance and steadfast faithfulness from His people. History unfolds under God's sovereign control, ensuring that evil does not prevail over the Church. Jesus will return in all His glory to execute final judgment on the wicked and grant eternal blessings to the righteous who persevere.

## NOTABLE & POPULAR

**People**

John, the Beast, the Dragon

**Places**

Patmos, the seven churches

**Events**

Letters to Seven Churches, End Times Visions, New Heaven and Earth

**Verses**

**Revelation 1:19** Therefore write down the things you have seen, and the things that are, and the things that will happen after this.

**Revelation 13:16** And the second beast required all people small and great, rich and poor, free and slave, to receive a mark on their right hand or on their forehead,

**Revelation 19:11** Then I saw heaven standing open, and there before me was a white horse. And its rider is called Faithful and True. With righteousness He judges and wages war.

**Revelation 21:4** 'He will wipe away every tear from their eyes,' and there will be no more death or mourning or crying or pain, for the former things have passed away."

# Acknowledgments:

Free: Bible icons for all 66 books
by Jeffrey Kranz
https://overviewbible.com/free-bible-icons/#download

The Berean Standard Bible
Placed into the public domain as of April 30, 2023
https://berean.bible

## Suggested Websites for Online Study:

https://www.gotquestions.org

https://www.intouch.org

https://bibleproject.com

https://www.bible.com

https://biblehub.com

https://thirdmill.org

# More from Elkleaf Publishing:

The Revival Team Series by Deakon Reeves

Faith and Adventure Fiction

Available wherever books are sold

Get the Series Prequel Free at elkleafpublishing.com

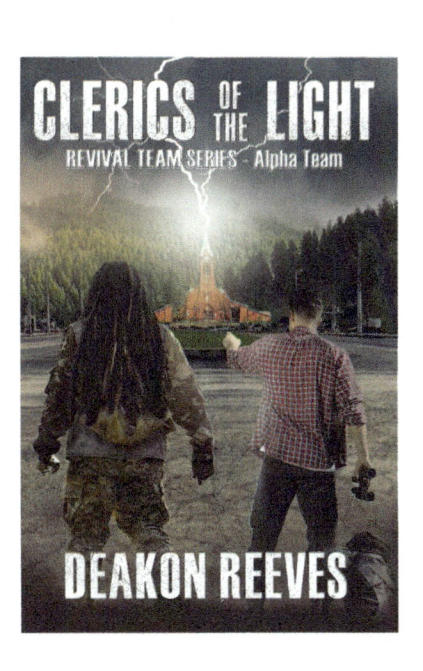

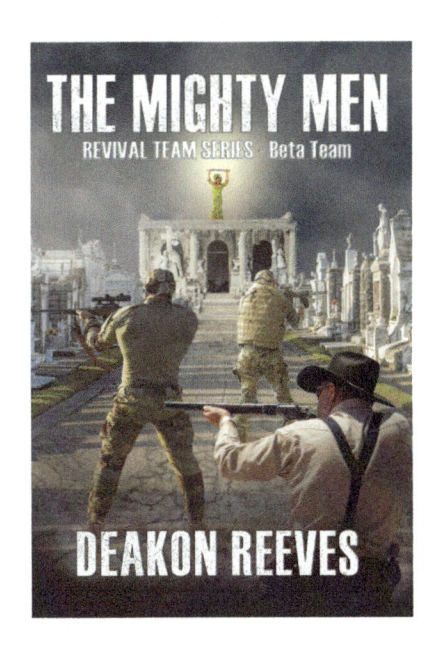

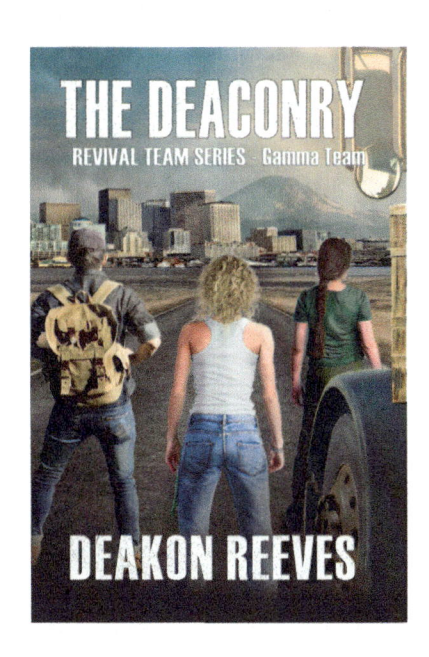